SCHOLASTIC

NAVIGATING NONFICTION

by Alice Boynton and Wiley Blevins

D1546955

Excepting those portions intended for classroom use, no part of this publication may be reproduced in whole or in part, or stored in a retrieval system, or transmitted in any form or by any means, electronic, mechanical, photocopying, recording, or otherwise, without written permission of the publisher. For information regarding permission, write to Scholastic Inc., 557 Broadway, New York, NY 10012. Scholastic Inc. grants teachers who have purchased *Navigating Nonfiction* permission to reproduce from this book those pages intended for use in their classrooms. Notice of copyright must appear on all copies of copyrighted materials.

Credits appear on page 111 which constitutes an extension of this copyright page.

Copyright © 2007 by Scholastic Inc. All rights reserved. Published by Scholastic Inc. Printed in the U.S.A.

ISBN-13 978-0-439-78295-1
ISBN-10 0-439-78295-3

SCHOLASTIC and associated logos and designs are trademarks and/or registered trademarks of Scholastic Inc.

1 2 3 4 5 6 7 8 9 10   66   15 14 13 12 11 10 09 08 07

Table of Contents

UNIT 7

Text Feature: Graphs

Text Structure: Compare/Contrast

UNIT 8

Text Feature: Time Lines

Text Structure: Problem/Solution

UNIT 9

Text Feature: Charts

Text Structure: Cause/Effect

UNIT 10

Text Feature: Maps

Text Structure: Description

ADDITIONAL MATERIALS

Graphic Organizers

Reading Nonfiction

Nonfiction gives you information. And it gives you information in many different ways. There's the main article, of course. But there may also be added information in photos, captions, labels, and sidebars. Sometimes when you look at the page, there's so much stuff on it you don't know where to begin! Let's see how to navigate the page.

Step 1 **Preview the article to get set for what you will read.** The title, introduction, and the added information clearly show that you will read about penguins.

Step 2 **Read the article.** This article is about a problem some penguins faced and an unusual solution.

Step 3 **Read the added information.** The photo and caption tell you about the effects of another oil spill. The sidebar gives you facts about two kinds of penguins. This is new information, not in the article.

Practice Your Skills!

1. Circle the title.

2. Underline new information in the photo caption.

3. Which penguins did you learn about in the sidebar?

PAIR SHARE How did you navigate the article?

PENGUiN PULLOVERS

Some penguins are now wearing pullover sweaters. The sweaters protect the penguins—but not from the cold!

These penguins live in South Africa. The one on the right is covered in oil from a spill there. It could use a sweater!

Penguin pullovers may look funny, but they're no laughing matter. They protect the birds from the dangers of oil spills. When oil comes in contact with penguin feathers, it takes away the birds' natural oils. Those natural oils are needed to keep the penguins warm and dry in icy waters.

Penguins also **preen**, or clean their feathers with their beaks. The sweaters keep the penguins from swallowing the harmful oil from the spill when they're preening.

After an oil spill near Australia, rescue workers fitted the penguins with doll sweaters. The idea worked so well that an environmental group asked people everywhere to start knitting. Soon, they had more than 5,000 sweaters!

Penguin Picks

There are 17 kinds of penguins in the world. Here are two.

Emperor penguins are the largest in the world. At 4 feet tall and 83 pounds, they're bigger than many third graders!

Chinstrap penguins look like they're wearing helmets. They all have a line of black feathers that look like straps under their chins.

Before You Read

Preview the article. Check (✔) the special features it has.

___ title
___ photos
___ map
___ headings
___ caption
___ pronunciation guide

As You Read

• Did you read the title and headings?
❑ Yes ❑ No

• Did you figure out how to pronounce *ASIMO?*
❑ Yes ❑ No

• Did you understand what a *device* is?
❑ Yes ❑ No

• How did you navigate the page?

After You Read

1. Why are robots good workers?

2. What are three new facts you learned?

 PAIR SHARE How do you think robots will help people in the future?

MARVELOUS MACHINES

Scientists are building new robots that can do many jobs for people—on Earth and in outer space.

Rescue Robots

Robots can do jobs that are too dangerous or difficult for people to do. Search-and-rescue robots were created to save lives after a **disaster**. These robots are the size of a shoebox. They can go places where humans and rescue dogs don't fit. For example, after an earthquake, the robots can roll deep into rubble, or broken pieces of stone and brick. They can detect, or notice, human breath, which helps them find survivors.

The robot arm pours a cup of tea.

REAL ROBOT

It climbs stairs, dances, and even plays soccer! At four feet tall, it looks like a kid in a spacesuit. It is a new type of robot called ASIMO (AH-see-moh).

ASIMO can greet a person when he or she approaches. It can recognize a waving hand and wave back. ASIMO also recognizes its name. When someone calls its name, it turns toward that person.

The creators of ASIMO hope that the robot will be able to help fight fires and that it can be an aide to the disabled.

A Robot Astronaut

A robot called Robonaut will someday go into space with astronauts. Robonaut has a hand that can use tools. The handy robot will perform dangerous jobs such as repairing the spacecraft.

Robot Aides

Other robots are now being built to help disabled people. One company is working on a robot arm. This **device**, or machine, will pick up objects for people who can't use their own hands.

On Your Own

Read the sidebar below. Then draw a robot that you imagine can be used to explore one of the places in the article. When you're finished, write a caption under your illustration.

Robots Explore Extremes

Exploration has come a long way since Christopher Columbus! Today, with the help of robots, exploration continues on land, underwater, and in space.

Under the Sea

The seas are filled with ancient buried cities and sunken ships. Scientists are working on a robot fish that may help them explore these underwater treasures. The robot fish, named Wanda, is based on a real fish called a pike. A pike can move and turn very fast. Scientists hope that making Wanda will help them figure out how to make underwater vessels that can move and turn very quickly.

Mission to Mars

Scientists at NASA sent two robots, named Spirit and Opportunity, to Mars. The robots spent each day searching for signs of water along the ground and inside rocks. The robots had special tools to drill through rocks.

Really Cool Place

Antarctica is Earth's driest, windiest, and coldest continent. Each October, when the weather in Antarctica starts to get less cold, many scientists visit there to study its icebergs and glaciers. They also study its life forms, such as penguins and seals. Robots will be very useful in Antarctica. They won't be bothered by the cold!

Reading Nonfiction

As you know, nonfiction gives you information about a topic. And it does this in many different ways. Most of the information is in the main article. But there is also **added information** in photos, captions, labels, and sidebars. Where do you begin?

Step 1 **Preview the article to get set for what you will read.** The title, headings, and the added information tell you that you will read about a new museum.

Step 2 **Read the article.** This article is about the opening of a museum to honor Native Americans.

Step 3 **Read the added information.** The photo and caption tell you how the people celebrated. The sidebar shows some of the objects in the museum. This is new information, not in the article.

Practice Your Skills!

1. Circle the title and each heading.

2. Put a check (✔) next to the feature you read last.

3. Underline the sentence that tells you there are Native Americans living in all parts of the U.S.

PAIR SHARE What are the different ways the author presents information about this topic?

A NEW MUSEUM

Many of the people marched and danced to beating drums, jangling bells, and chirping flutes. Dancers wore bright feathers, masks, and headdresses up to two feet tall.

A Reason to Celebrate

On a sunny fall day in 2004, people from all over the country came to Washington, D.C. They were there to celebrate the opening of the Smithsonian National Museum of the American Indian. The museum honors Native American cultures. Visitors to the museum learn about the history, languages, traditions, and art of many different Native American tribes.

Past, Present, and Future

Inside the museum, visitors can look at sculptures, baskets, blankets, musical instruments, tools, and other objects from Native American life. Today, there are more than 4 million Native Americans living throughout the U.S. They hope that the new museum will help their cultures and history live on in the future.

Art and Objects

Take a look at some of the artifacts inside the new museum.

Moccasins
These shoes (above), made with leather and glass beads, were worn by Cheyenne (SHY-an) Indians in Oklahoma in the 1870s.

Totem Pole
A Tlingit (TLING-git) carver from Alaska created this 20-foot totem pole for the museum.

Practice Your Skills!

Before You Read

Preview the article. Check (✔) the special features it has.

___ headings
___ map
___ time line
___ captions
___ pronunciation guide

As You Read

- Did you use the title and headings to figure out what the article was about?
  ❏ Yes ❏ No

- Did you find the Iditarod route on the map?
  ❏ Yes ❏ No

- Did you look at the photos carefully?
  ❏ Yes ❏ No

- Explain how you navigated the page.

After You Read

1. Why is the Iditarod not just a sport for the Seaveys?

2. What do Alaskans and Native Americans want people to learn about them?

PAIR SHARE What new information did you learn from the photo, map, and sidebar?

SNOW DOGS

Taking care of just one dog can be hard. Think how hard it must be for the Seavey family. They own and take care of more than 70 dogs!

The Seaveys train their dogs to pull sleds in races. The most famous race is the Alaskan **Iditarod** (eye-DIT-uh-rod). The Iditarod features teams of 12 to 16 dogs that pull sleds across a long trail of 1,100 miles. The **route** runs from Anchorage to Nome. The dogs' owners, called *mushers*, travel with them on this long trek, or journey. Mushers ride on the sled and guide the dogs along the trail. It takes almost two weeks to finish the route.

A Family Business

For the Seaveys, the race is more than a sport. "This is how we make our living," says Mitch Seavey. "It's like a family farm." Mitch and his sons train, feed, and clean up after the dogs.

History of the Iditarod

Until the early 1900s, the only way to travel in Alaska during winter was by dogsled. The Iditarod honors a famous dogsled trip that happened in 1925. That winter, many people in Alaska became ill. Dogsled teams rushed medicine across 700 miles to save the people's lives. The trail they rushed across is used for the Iditarod. This race is a way of keeping Alaska's history alive. And the Seaveys are among many people who are helping.

DOG SAFETY

The Seaveys take steps to make sure their dogs are safe during every race.

▲ **During races, the dogs wear booties to protect their paws from ice and rocks.**

▲ **Tyrell Seavey puts a harness on his dog. It connects the dog to the sled. It's padded to keep the dog comfortable.**

◄ **The dogs nap during rest stops. The Seaveys spread hay on the ground to keep the dogs warm and dry.**

On Your Own

Look at this page of nonfiction. Notice all the features. How would you read the page? List the steps you would take. What would you read first? Then what?

First, I will _____
_____.

Next, I will _____
_____.

Last, I will _____
_____.

Blind Musher
Takes on the Iditarod

Jagged mountains. Frozen rivers. Finger-numbing temperatures. For any musher, the Iditarod is a super-hard race. But Rachael Scdoris is no ordinary musher. She is blind.

Try, Try Again

Even though she is blind, Rachael began mushing when she was very young. But her father would not allow her to go out on a run by herself. Finally, he gave in. Rachael ran her first race when she was 11 years old. And she has been racing ever since.

The Biggest Race of All

This year, Rachael will be at the starting line in Anchorage, Alaska, to race in the Iditarod. She will have a visual interpreter at her side. His job will just be to tell Rachael about dangers that she won't be able to see. For example, a low tree branch or a sharp turn ahead could be disaster. Rachael says, "When he says duck, I'll duck immediately!"

Rachael says that she doesn't want to be known as "the blind musher." Instead, she would like to be known as "the good musher with fast dogs."

Mushers say that dogs have sharper senses than humans do. They can find their way on trails they've never been on before.

All About Alaska

- Alaska borders on two oceans and three seas. It has 3,000 rivers and about 3 million lakes.
- More animals than people live in Alaska.

Problem/Solution

Practice Your Skills!

Before You Read

Vocabulary Read the related words. Use them to fill in the chart. Then add other words to each box.

invent   inventor   invention

Person	Action	Thing

As You Read

Text Structure The article tells about inventions that were **solutions** to **problems**. As you read, look for signal words such as *because of* and *as a result*. They will be followed by solutions to the problem. Circle the signal words.

Text Feature Why do you think the writer added the sidebar?

After You Read

1. What problems might Shannon Crabill's invention solve?

2. What do the boldfaced words in the article mean?

3. Which invention described in the article do you think is the most useful? Why?

KID Inventors

BAT BOY

One day, Jacob Dunnack, 8, forgot to bring a ball to play baseball. Instead of getting upset, his problem gave him an idea for an **invention**. Jacob came up with the "JD Bat Ball," a bat that holds baseballs.

Jacob asked his dad to help him design the bat. Together, they created a bat with a removable cap. This lets a batter store balls inside the bat. Therefore, the player can't forget to bring a ball.

Jacob sold his invention to a toy store. As a result, all kids can remember to have a ball!

READY, SET, INVENT!

Have you ever had a problem you wanted to fix? Most great inventions begin with a problem and end with a solution. These simple steps and examples will help you turn a problem into a cool invention!

1

Think of a problem that needs a solution.

Example: You keep losing pens and pencils or forget to bring them to school.

These kid inventors prove that you're never too young to have a great idea.

HELMET HELPER

When Michael Marsal and Margaret Winter were 11 years old, they invented a new helmet. Michael says, "I went to hockey camp with a kid who was deaf. He couldn't hear the whistles to stop and go during the game. I wanted to do something to help him."

Margaret says, "We designed a helmet with two lights in front. Red was for stop, and green was for go. The coach or referee could use a remote control to flash one of the lights on the helmet. But we couldn't get all the parts we needed to make the helmet. A company agreed to make a model for us."

The model worked perfectly. Then, the two kids got a **patent**. A patent shows that you own an idea. No one else can copy that idea and take credit for it.

Both Michael and Margaret agree that any kid can come up with a good invention. It just has to be an **original** idea, something new that solves a problem that you or other people have.

TIME IN

Shannon Crabill, 12, has perfect timing. She learned about a kid-inventor contest and decided to enter it. Shannon wanted her invention to be fun and useful. She thought of a problem that lots of people have. Then, she came up with a cool clock that she named "Talk Time."

"Talk Time" is an alarm clock with a built-in microphone that lets you record your own message. You can speak, sing, or play music into it. When the alarm goes off, it plays back your message.

Shannon's clock sounded great. It won first prize!

2
Come up with an invention that would solve the problem.
Example: A pen-and-pencil belt.

3
List the materials you'll need to create the invention.
Example: An old belt, glue, Velcro,™ pens, and pencils.

4
Describe how your invention will work.
Example: Pieces of Velcro™ are glued to the belt, pens, and pencils. This lets the pens and pencils stick to the belt until they are needed.

Problem/Solution

Reread the article. Fill in the graphic organizer. For each invention, tell what the problem was. Then tell how the invention solved the problem.

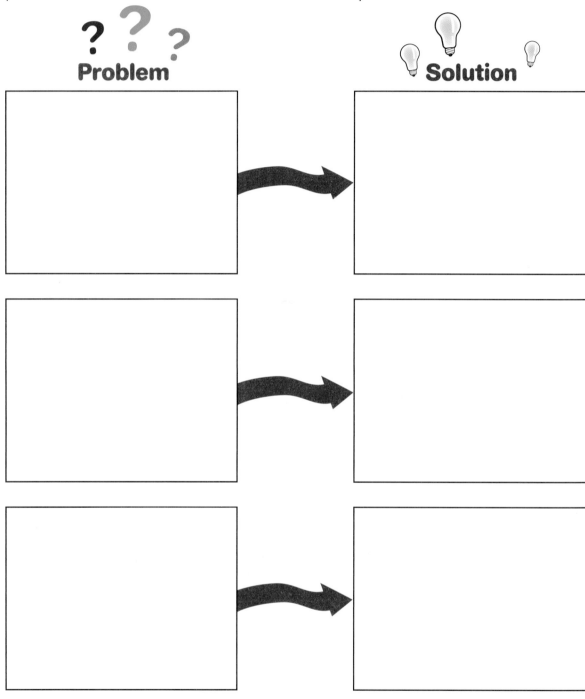

? ? ?
Problem

Solution

 Retell Use the chart above to retell the information from "Kid Inventors" in your own words.

Writing Frame

Use the information in your graphic organizer to fill in the writing frame.

Most inventions solve problems. Here are some examples.

One problem was that _____

_____. This problem was solved when Jacob invented

_____.

Another problem was that _____

_____

_____. This problem was solved when Michael and Margaret

invented a _____

_____.

Another problem was that _____

_____. This problem was solved when

Shannon invented _____

_____.

 Use the writing frame above as a model to write a paragraph about another invention that solved a problem. Look in your science book if you need facts about inventors and their inventions.

Nonfiction Features

Most nonfiction books, such as your science and social studies textbooks, contain many features. What are they and why are they there?

- The chapter **title** tells you what the topic is.
- The **introduction** and **headings** tell you the main ideas.
- **Graphic aids**, such as charts, illustrate facts in the text or add information.
- **Boldface type** signals important words to remember.
- **Pronunciation guides** help you say words you may not have heard before.

Now find these features in the article below.

Practice Your Skills!

1. Put an **X** on the title.

2. Underline the three main headings.

3. Circle the sidebar information.

PAIR SHARE What does the heart do? How does it keep you alive?

Be Heart Smart!

You are heart smart when you stay active and eat well. Let's learn about what your heart does and how you can keep your heart healthy.

Heart

Did you know that your **heart** is about the size of your fist? This muscle is very busy. It never stops working. Your heart works like a pump. It pumps blood through every part of your body. Your blood moves through thin tubes called **blood vessels**.

Your Heart Keeps Beating

You can feel your heart beat every time your heart muscle tightens and relaxes. When you exercise, your heart beats faster. This makes your heart work hard and become strong. That's why you should be active every day!

Arteries

Arteries are a kind of blood vessel. Arteries carry blood *away* from your heart.

Veins

Veins (vaynz) are another kind of blood vessel. Veins bring blood *back* to the heart.

Did You Know?

It takes about 45 seconds for blood to travel around your whole body. This is called **circulation** because blood circles your body.

Practice Your Skills!

Before You Read

Preview the article. Check (✔) the special features it has.

_____ headings
_____ boldfaced words
_____ map
_____ caption
_____ sidebar

As You Read

- Did you read the title of the article to learn the topic?
  ❏ Yes ❏ No

- Did you read the headings to learn the main ideas?
  ❏ Yes ❏ No

- Did you find out the meanings of the words in boldface?
  ❏ Yes ❏ No

- Explain how you read the article.

After You Read

1. What does _foraging_ mean?

2. Why did scientists put sensors into the bees' hives?

PAIR SHARE What about bees surprises you? What interesting facts about bees did you learn?

New Buzz on Bees

A honeybee wears an electronic tag attached to its body. Experts use the tag to track bees' comings and goings. The tags don't harm the bees.

Honeybees are not just great at making honey. Experts say they are also great detectives. Now, the experts are working with honeybees on a big case. The bees are being used to locate areas of pollution.

Seeing Is Bee-lieving

Honeybees have fuzzy bodies that act like magnets. While the bees are **foraging**, or searching for food, all kinds of things get stuck to their bodies. Even invisible and odorless chemicals can get stuck to them. Then, it all gets carried back to the bees' hives.

Sometimes, the bees collect **pollutants**, or things that make dirty water, air, and soil. A team of experts place special machines called _sensors_ into the hives. When the bees return, the sensors can tell if the bees are carrying pollutants.

When dangerous pollutants are found, the experts track where the bees went to forage. This tells the experts where the pollutants came from. The experts know which areas need to be cleaned up.

So far, the bees have helped locate pollution in nearly 30 areas across the country. That has the team buzzing with excitement.

Sweet Stuff

People have used honey as a food since ancient times. Read the steps below to learn how bees make honey.

Honey is made from **nectar**, a sugar-filled, watery liquid. The bees sip nectar from flowers (see above) and carry it to their hives. The nectar is stored in a pouch that each honeybee has, called a **honey stomach**.

Inside the beehive, the bees build **honeycombs**. A honeycomb is made up of tiny, six-sided cells. The bees release the nectar into the empty cells of the honeycomb (see above).

In the honeycomb, water in the nectar begins to **evaporate**, or change from a liquid to a gas. The nectar starts to become thick and sticky. When enough water evaporates, the thick nectar is called honey.

On Your Own

First, read this article about ants. Then fill in the missing text features.

- Write a title.
- Write a heading for each section.
- Write a description of a photo or picture you'd like to include. Add a caption.

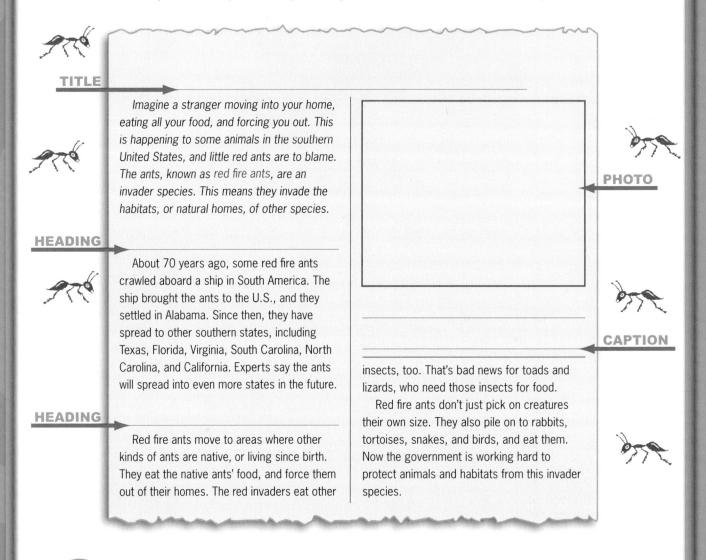

TITLE

Imagine a stranger moving into your home, eating all your food, and forcing you out. This is happening to some animals in the southern United States, and little red ants are to blame. The ants, known as red fire ants, are an invader species. This means they invade the habitats, or natural homes, of other species.

HEADING

About 70 years ago, some red fire ants crawled aboard a ship in South America. The ship brought the ants to the U.S., and they settled in Alabama. Since then, they have spread to other southern states, including Texas, Florida, Virginia, South Carolina, North Carolina, and California. Experts say the ants will spread into even more states in the future.

HEADING

Red fire ants move to areas where other kinds of ants are native, or living since birth. They eat the native ants' food, and force them out of their homes. The red invaders eat other insects, too. That's bad news for toads and lizards, who need those insects for food.

Red fire ants don't just pick on creatures their own size. They also pile on to rabbits, tortoises, snakes, and birds, and eat them. Now the government is working hard to protect animals and habitats from this invader species.

PHOTO

CAPTION

Ask yourself, "What additional facts could be included in a sidebar?" List them.

_____

_____

_____

Nonfiction Features

Many textbooks and other nonfiction books contain features that make the information easier to understand. Here's how to use the features.

Step 1 **Read the title to find out what the topic is.**
The title tells that this article will be about a woman who lives with chimpanzees.

Step 2 **Read the introduction. It tells you the main idea.**
This introduction tells who Jane Goodall is and what she does that is so special.

Step 3 **Look at the headings.** The headings show the main idea of each section.

Step 4 **Look for graphic aids.** The **map** shows where Jane lived and worked. The **photo** shows Jane at work.

Step 5 **Look for boldfaced words and pronunciation guides.**
Boldfaced words are the key words to remember. Pronunciation guides tell you how to say a word.

Practice Your Skills!

1. Put an **X** on the title of the article.

2. Circle the headings in the article.

3. Underline one fact under each heading.

 PAIR SHARE Why is Jane Goodall an important person to read about?

Jane Goodall
Living With Chimpanzees

Jane Goodall is a famous **scientist** who has spent her life learning about chimpanzees. She has watched them as they eat, play, and live their daily lives. She has learned a lot about how they act and how they use sticks and grass tools to catch and eat food.

Jane around them. They began to trust her and behave in normal ways. Some even began to treat her as if she was a member of their family.

Africa
Tanzania

Jane's Life in Tanzania

Over 40 years ago, Jane traveled to Tanzania (tan-zuh-NEE-uh) in Africa. There she lived in a big **game reserve** with the chimpanzees. The game reserve was a protected place where no hunters were allowed and she could study the chimpanzees freely. Over time, the chimpanzees began to feel comfortable with having

Jane's Work As a Scientist

Goodall spent many years **observing**, or carefully watching, these chimpanzees. She has written many articles and books.

Jane **founded**, or began, an organization called the Jane Goodall Institute. It raises money to teach people about the chimpanzees and to help prevent the destruction of the forests in which these chimpanzees live.

Practice Your Skills!

Before You Read

Preview the article.
Check (✔) the special
features it has.

_____ headings
_____ caption
_____ map
_____ graph
_____ photo
_____ boldfaced words

As You Read

• Did you read the
  title and headings
  to learn the main
  ideas?
  ❏ Yes ❏ No

• Did you find
  and read all the
  boldfaced words?
  ❏ Yes ❏ No

• Circle your state
  on the map.

• Explain how you
  read the article.

After You Read

1. Where does Ben
Kilham live? What two
ways did you use to
find out this fact?

2. What is another
word for *understand*
in the article?

PAIR SHARE What do you
think are the
pros and cons of Ben's
job? Why?

MOTHER BEAR MAN

New Hampshire

Ben Kilham is wild about bears. This bear expert has been training and saving orphaned black bear cubs in New Hampshire for ten years. Black bear cubs **rely**, or depend, on their mothers to teach them how to survive in the wild. Without a mother to guide them, cubs have a difficult time getting by. That's where Ben steps in.

DEN MOTHER

Ben raises the orphaned cubs in his own home. He spends lots of time with them, just like a mother bear would.

Ben also teaches life skills to the cubs, such as how to find food. He takes them through forests to show them leaves and other foods to eat. How does he make the bear cubs **comprehend**, or understand, that they've found food? He get s down and chomps on the leaves himself! The cubs then copy him. Dinner is served!

BEAR FACTS

• Not all black bears are black. They can be brown, blond, or white. Some even look a little blue!

• Bear cubs usually stay with their mother for about 17 months.

• A female bear is called a **solar** and a male bear is called a **boar**. This causes some people to think that bears are related to pigs! However, bears and pigs are not related.

• Hibernating black bears can go without eating or drinking for about 100 days!

BACK TO THE WILD

Thanks to Ben, many cubs also learn how to spot enemies and avoid places where they could get hurt. Once the cubs are ready to be on their own, "Mother Bear Man" sends them back to the wild.

On Your Own

Read this article about a scientist. Then fill in the missing text features.

- Write a title.

- Write a heading for each section.

- Write a description of a photo or illustration you'd like to include. Add a caption.

_____
[Title]

Susan Hendrickson made the dinosaur find of the century, a period of 100 years. She found a 67-million-year-old Tyrannosaurus rex skeleton—the largest, most complete one ever found.

_____
[Heading]

"It all began with a flat tire," Susan Hendrickson explained. All summer in 1990, she and a team of fossil hunters searched for dinosaur remains in South Dakota. "We slept outside for two months. I was tired by then," Hendrickson recalls. The team decided to pack up and drive away, but their truck had a flat tire. It would take half a day to fix it.

Hendrickson decided to search one more area. While searching, she saw some bones sticking out of a hill. Within minutes, she knew they were T. rex bones. "It was stupendous. All the bones were intact," Hendrickson said. Her team named the dinosaur "Sue" in her honor.

_____
[Heading]

Experts spent months **assembling,** or putting together, more than 300 bones of the skeleton. When completed, the Field Museum in Chicago put the T. rex skeleton on display for the world to marvel at. "Sue has waited 67 million years for this," said Hendrickson.

[Photo or Illustration]

_____
_____
[Caption]

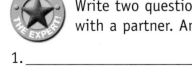

Write two questions about the article. When you're done, change papers with a partner. Answer each other's questions.

1. _____

_____

2. _____

_____

Compare/Contrast

Practice Your Skills!

Before You Read

Vocabulary Read these important words from the article. Tell how the two words in each pair are related. Use the pairs in a sentence that shows what they mean.

Related Word Pairs
extinct/species
expert/discovered
existed/extinct

As You Read

Text Structure The author of this article **compares and contrasts** dinosaurs and dinosaur discoveries. As you read, ask yourself, "What is the same about these two dinosaurs?" to compare them. Ask yourself, "What is different about these two dinosaurs?" to contrast them.

Text Features What text features did the author include in the article? How did they help you read and better understand the article?

After You Read

1. What is special about each dinosaur discovery in the article?

2. Why are dinosaurs a good topic for movies?

3. What do you know about dinosaur discoveries? Tell about dinosaurs you have read about or seen in a museum, on TV, or in the movies.

DINO TIME

Dinosaurs became extinct about 65 million years ago. Now, they are back in a big way. Dinosaurs haven't come back to life, but this past year, they made big news.

Oldest Bones

About five years ago, experts announced that they had found very special dinosaur fossils in Madagascar. The fossils are believed to be the oldest dinosaur remains ever discovered— 230 million years old. This old-timer was a plant eater, about the size of a kangaroo.

Experts search for dinosaur fossils in Argentina. The remains of many dinosaurs have been found in that area of the world.

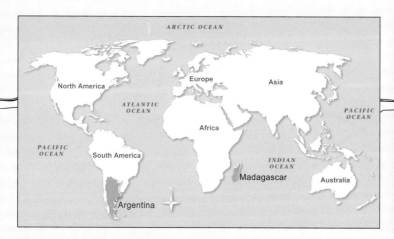

A boy gets a look inside the mouth of a T. rex.

Bigger Than the T. Rex

Around the same time, experts announced the discovery of a new meat-eating species of dinosaur in Argentina. This large lizard was about 45 feet long, which means it was even bigger than the Tyrannosaurus rex. It is now believed to be the biggest of all meat-eating dinosaurs.

Dinos on the Big Screen

Dinosaurs are so **popular**, or liked by many people, that they are the subject of many movies. The dinosaur movie *Jurassic Park* is one of the most successful movies of all time.

Why are dinosaurs so popular? Expert Paul Sereno says, "We are very interested in animals that existed in the past. We wonder how they lived and what it would be like if they were still on Earth."

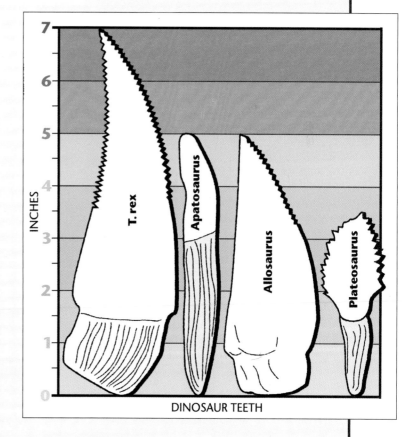

INCHES

7
6
5
4
3
2
1
0

T. rex

Apatosaurus

Allosaurus

Plateosaurus

DINOSAUR TEETH

Compare/Contrast

Reread "Dino Time." Fill in the graphic organizer to compare and contrast the dinosaur finds in Madagascar and Argentina. Tell how they are the same and how they are different.

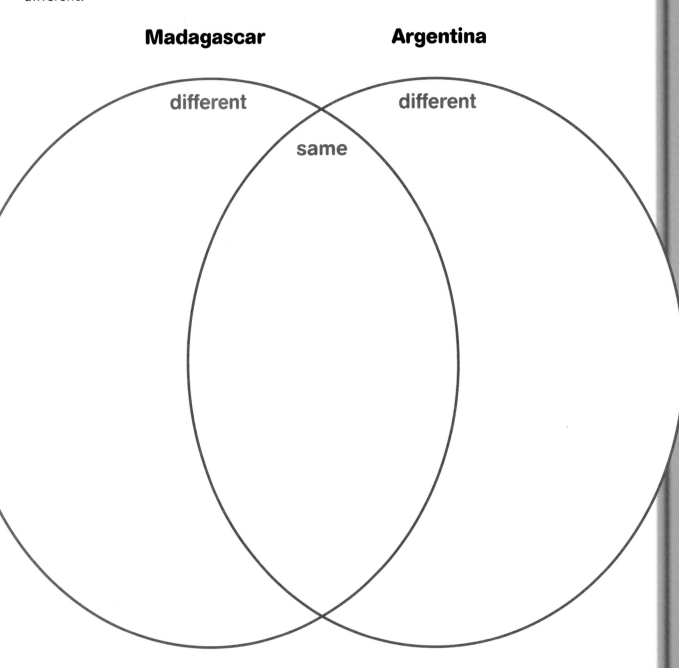

Madagascar

Argentina

different

different

same

 Retell Use the graphic organizer above to retell "Dino Time" in your own words. Remember to include how the different dinosaur finds are alike and different.

Writing Frame

Use the information in your graphic organizer to fill in the writing frame.

Both the dinosaur find in Madagascar and the dinosaur find in Argentina are

the same in some ways. They are the same because they both _____

_____

_____.

In some ways, though, the dinosaur find in Madagascar and the dinosaur

find in Argentina are different. They are different because _____

_____

_____

_____.

So, the dinosaur find in Madagascar and the dinosaur find in Argentina

have both similarities and differences.

 Use the writing frame above as a model to compare and contrast other types of animals, such as amphibians and reptiles. Look in your science textbook if you need facts that will help you fill in the frame.

Diagrams

Many science books contain diagrams to go with the text. A **diagram** is a special picture that shows the parts of something or a process. For example, a diagram can show the parts of a plant or the phases of the moon. The diagram helps you "picture" the information and makes it easier to understand. Here's how to read a diagram.

Step 1 **Read the title to find out what the diagram shows.**
The diagram below shows the underground homes of gophers living near the Mount St. Helens volcano.

Step 2 **Read the labels. They name parts of the diagram.**
Some of the labels in this diagram also give details about the gophers' underground homes.

Step 3 **Follow the line or arrow from the label to the diagram.**
Each label is near the part of the diagram it describes.

Practice Your Skills!

1. Put an **X** on the name of the gophers' underground home.

2. Circle the names of the food that gophers eat.

3. What other animals live in the gophers' homes?

PAIR SHARE Why are the gophers' homes good shelters during a volcano's explosion?

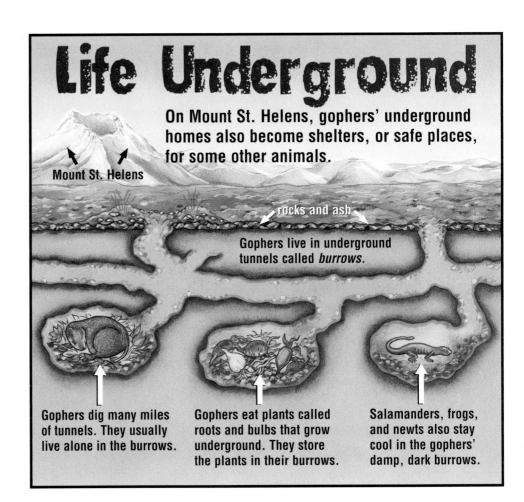

Life Underground

On Mount St. Helens, gophers' underground homes also become shelters, or safe places, for some other animals.

Mount St. Helens

rocks and ash

Gophers live in underground tunnels called *burrows*.

Gophers dig many miles of tunnels. They usually live alone in the burrows.

Gophers eat plants called roots and bulbs that grow underground. They store the plants in their burrows.

Salamanders, frogs, and newts also stay cool in the gophers' damp, dark burrows.

Practice Your Skills!

Before You Read
Preview the article. Check (✔) the special features it has.

_____ title
_____ headings
_____ map
_____ photo
_____ pronunciations
_____ diagram

As You Read
- Did you read the title of the diagram?
  ❏ Yes ❏ No

- Did you read each label?
  ❏ Yes ❏ No

- Did you connect each label to a part of the picture?
  ❏ Yes ❏ No

- Explain how you read the diagram.

After You Read
1. What causes the magma to burst out of the volcano?

2. What is the name of the hot liquid that flows down the side of a volcano?

PAIR SHARE What effect can a volcanic eruption have on the nearby plants, animals, and people?

HOT SPOT

Vesuvius last erupted in 1944. People live near the volcano because the soil is rich and good for growing crops such as grapes, tomatoes, onions, oranges, and lemons.

The people who live near Mount Vesuvius (vuh-SOO-vee-uhs) must be ready to leave the area at any time. Why? Vesuvius, a huge volcano, may soon **erupt**, or explode. That means big trouble for those people—all 2 million of them!

FIRE FROM THE MOUNTAINS

If Vesuvius erupts, it will release hot gases, thick ashes, and **lava**, or red-hot liquid rock. It will be very dangerous for anyone to be nearby. "We expect that a large area could be destroyed in a few minutes," says Edoardo Del Pezzo, a volcano expert. This is what happened almost 2,000 years ago. An eruption by Vesuvius buried the **ancient**, or very old, city of Pompeii (pom-PAY).

ESCAPING THE ERUPTION

To make sure everyone can get to safety, special practice drills are held. When sirens are sounded, the people get to their cars quickly and drive away from the area.

Scientists are studying Vesuvius closely. They hope to know when the volcano will erupt before it happens.

HOW A VOLCANO ERUPTS

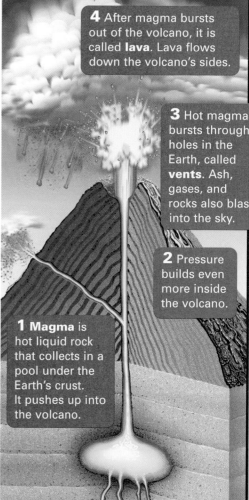

4 After magma bursts out of the volcano, it is called **lava**. Lava flows down the volcano's sides.

3 Hot magma bursts through holes in the Earth, called **vents**. Ash, gases, and rocks also blast into the sky.

2 Pressure builds even more inside the volcano.

1 Magma is hot liquid rock that collects in a pool under the Earth's crust. It pushes up into the volcano.

On Your Own

Look at the diagrams of three types of volcanoes. Think about how the information in each diagram adds to what you already know about volcanoes. Remember:

- Read the diagram's title and labels.

- Study the diagram carefully.

- Think about the information it shows. For example, ask yourself, "Which type of volcano is Mount St. Helens?"

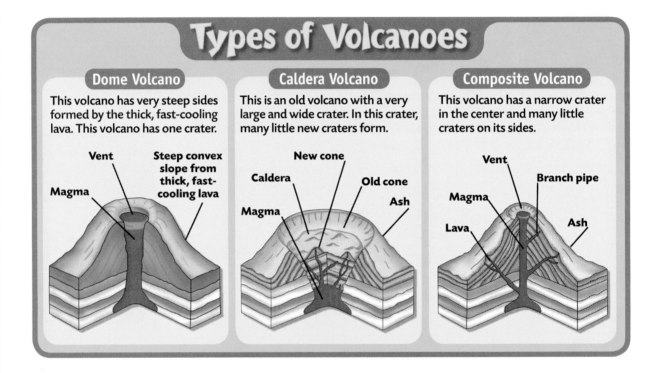

Types of Volcanoes

Dome Volcano
This volcano has very steep sides formed by the thick, fast-cooling lava. This volcano has one crater.

Vent
Steep convex slope from thick, fast-cooling lava
Magma

Caldera Volcano
This is an old volcano with a very large and wide crater. In this crater, many little new craters form.

New cone
Caldera
Old cone
Ash
Magma

Composite Volcano
This volcano has a narrow crater in the center and many little craters on its sides.

Vent
Branch pipe
Magma
Lava
Ash

Read the questions below. Put a ✔ in front of each question that can be answered by the diagram. Then, write another question about the diagram. When you're done, change papers with a partner. Answer each other's questions.

☐ 1. Which volcano has the widest cone?

☐ 2. Which volcanoes have more than one crater?

☐ 3. Was it hot in Memphis on March 7?

    4. My own question _____

_____

Diagrams

Nonfiction often contains diagrams to go with the text. A **diagram** is a special picture that shows the parts of something or a process. For example, a diagram can show how to set your digital watch. The diagram helps you "picture" the information and makes it easier to understand. Here's how:

Step 1 **Read the title to find out what the diagram shows.**
The diagram below shows the parts of a pioneer flatboat.

Step 2 **Read the labels. They name parts of the diagram.**
The labels below name the important parts of the flatboat. They also include information about the parts.

Step 3 **Follow the line from the label to the diagram.**
The lines connect the labels to the picture.

Pioneer Flatboat

Some pioneers used flatboats to travel on rivers. A whole family could live on one flatboat. At the end of their trip, they took apart the flatboat and used the wood to build a house on land.

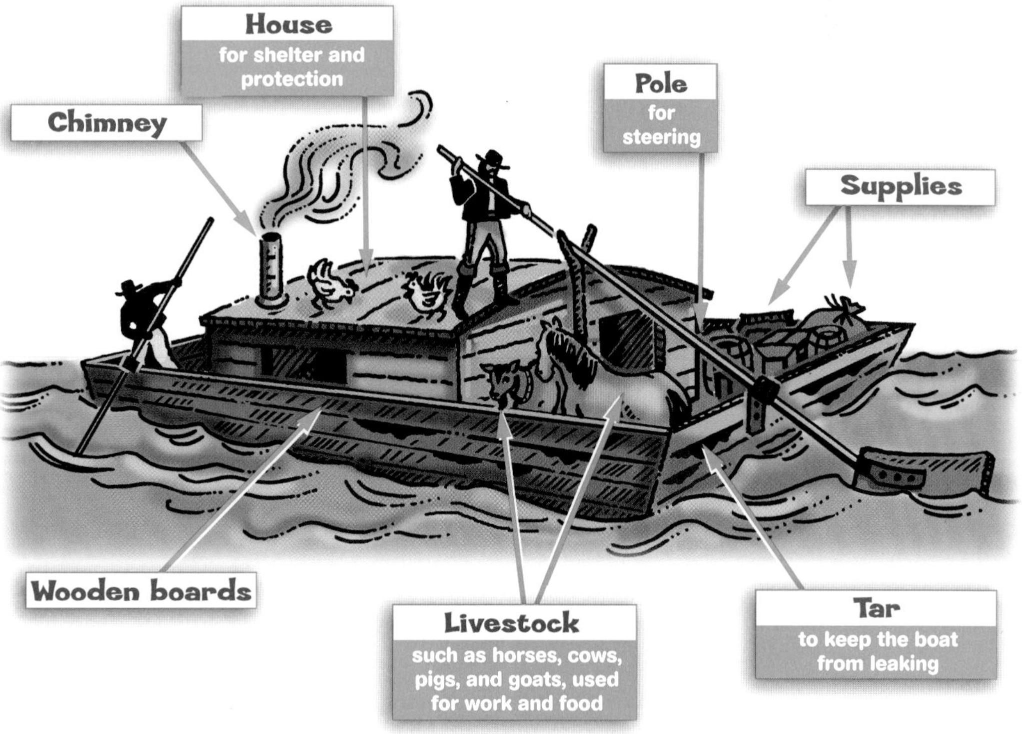

House
for shelter and protection

Chimney

Pole
for steering

Supplies

Wooden boards

Livestock
such as horses, cows, pigs, and goats, used for work and food

Tar
to keep the boat from leaking

Practice Your Skills!

1. Circle the labels that name parts of the flatboat.

2. Add a label on the dotted line.

3. Underline the word that means "farm animals used for work and food."

PAIR SHARE What were some of the advantages of a flatboat? Would you have liked to travel on one?

Before You Read

Preview the article. Check (✔) the special features it has.

_____ headings
_____ labels
_____ diagram
_____ caption
_____ boldfaced words

As You Read

- Did you read the title of the diagram?
  ❏ Yes ❏ No

- Did you read each label?
  ❏ Yes ❏ No

- Did you follow the line to the picture?
  ❏ Yes ❏ No

- Explain how you read the diagram.

After You Read

1. Why did the pioneers take so much with them?

2. What kind of person do you think a pioneer had to be?

PAIR SHARE What made the Conestoga wagon good for the long trip west?

The Way West

On the Oregon Trail People often move to new places to make a better life for themselves. In the 1840s, long before there were cars and trains, thousands of Americans left their homes in the East and the Midwest and went west. They traveled on the Oregon Trail to what was then a wilderness area. They hoped to build new homes and farm the land. They were **pioneers**, the first people to settle in a new area. The 2,000–mile trip along the Oregon Trail was difficult and dangerous. It took more than five months.

Wagon Trains Pioneers on the Oregon Trail traveled in wagon trains. A wagon train could have as many 1,000 people and more than 3,000 animals, such as cows and horses. Sometimes 100 wagons traveled together, stretching out for five miles. The large, creaking vehicles that took the pioneers west were **Conestoga** (con-iss-TOH-guh) **wagons**. A family would pack their wagon with flour, sugar, salt, bacon, coffee beans, spices, dried fruit, beans, rice, and more. It was important to be well prepared, because there weren't any stores along the way. They also carried pots, pans, a cast iron stove, a butter churn, furniture, and tools. All of those supplies added up to almost one ton of cargo—the same weight as an elephant!

Conestoga Wagon

Bows

Brake

Large wheel allows wagon to go over rocks.

Grease bucket so wheels can be oiled daily.

Cover is watertight to keep goods dry in the rain.

Wagon bed is watertight so it can float across rivers.

On Your Own

Here's a diagram of an object you probably see every day—a computer.

 Label the important parts of the computer.

 Then add some features to the diagram. Draw and label them. Remember to include a line from each label to the part that it names.

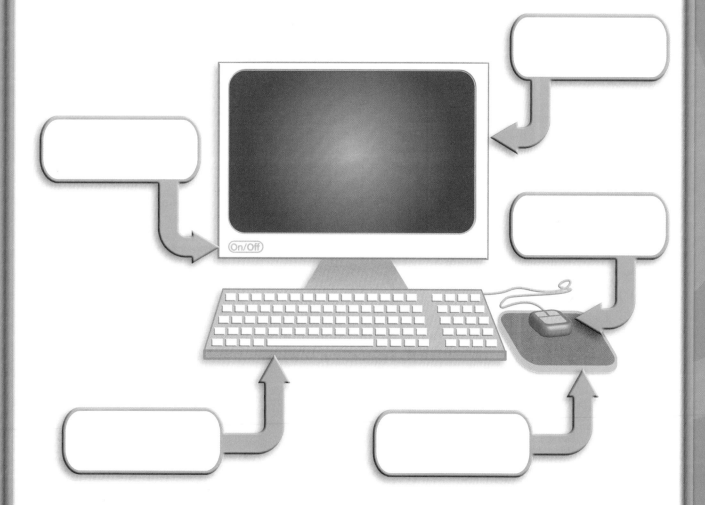

 Make a diagram of another common object, such as a telephone, DVD player, or bicycle. Be sure to label all the important features of the object.

LESSON 9

Text Structure

Description

Practice Your Skills!

Before You Read

Vocabulary Read the word pairs in the chart. Then write about how the two words are related.

Related Word Pairs	
prey hunter	
zone layer	
prey pray	

As You Read

Text Structure This article **describes** how animals in different zones of the ocean find food. The article contains many details.

Text Feature How does the diagram help you understand the article?

After You Read

1. Why is the Twilight Zone colder than the Sunlight Zone?

2. Study the diagram. What do you notice about the size of each zone as you go from the surface down to the ocean floor?

3. Which zone has the fewest animals? Why?

Discover the

The ocean is full of life, from its sunlit surface to its deep, dark bottom. How do creatures live and find food in these dark places? Their amazing bodies help.

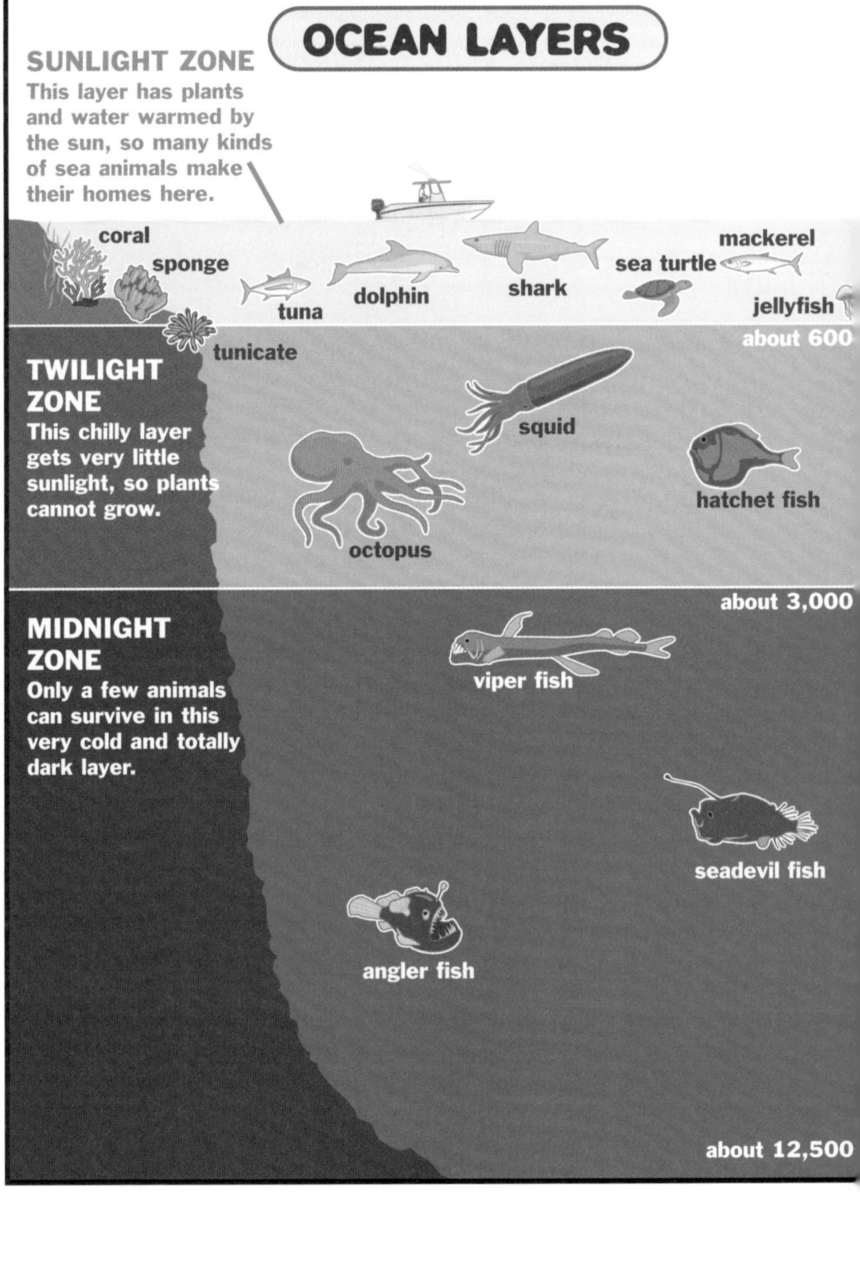

OCEAN LAYERS
SUNLIGHT ZONE
This layer has plants and water warmed by the sun, so many kinds of sea animals make their homes here.
coral
sponge
tuna
dolphin
shark
sea turtle
mackerel
jellyfish
about 600
tunicate
TWILIGHT ZONE
This chilly layer gets very little sunlight, so plants cannot grow.
squid
octopus
hatchet fish
about 3,000
MIDNIGHT ZONE
Only a few animals can survive in this very cold and totally dark layer.
viper fish
seadevil fish
angler fish
about 12,500

Deep

What big eyes you have!

Large eyes help deep-sea creatures search for food. The hatchet fish lives in the Twilight Zone. There is so little light here, our eyes would not be able to see anything at all.

However, hatchet fish have large eyes that can see in the dark waters. The eyes are on the top of the hatchet fish's head, so it can see and eat animals that swim above it.

What a bright light you have!

The seadevil fish swims in the Midnight Zone. It doesn't need big eyes like the hatchet fish has to find food. That's because it makes its own light, which helps it catch prey. A long body part, or **lure,** on the seadevil's head works a little like a fishing pole. The light on its end attracts other fish. When those fish swim in close, the seadevil eats them.

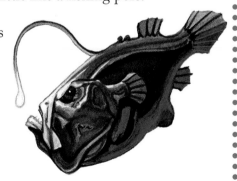

What big teeth you have!

Some fish in the Midnight Zone have big teeth that help them trap food. For example, viper fish's teeth are super-long and pointy. The viper fish catches prey in its mouth and chomps down. Then, the prey is trapped, like in a cage. Like some other fish in the Midnight Zone, at night the viper fish travels up into the Twilight Zone where food is more plentiful.

What a big mouth you have!

A big mouth also helps deep-sea animals catch food. This tunicate (TOO-ni-ket) lives on the ocean floor. It stays in one spot and keeps its mouth open. When prey swims inside, snap! The tunicate shuts its mouth and swallows.

Description

Reread "Discover the Deep." Fill in the chart with details that describe each ocean layer.

Ocean Layers

SUNLIGHT ZONE

Fact 1 _____

_____

_____

Fact 2 _____

_____

_____

TWILIGHT ZONE

Fact 1 _____

_____

_____

Fact 2 _____

_____

_____

MIDNIGHT ZONE

Fact 1 _____

_____

_____

Fact 2 _____

_____

_____

Retell Use the graphic organizer above to retell "Discover the Deep" in your own words. Include as much information as you can remember.

Writing Frame

Use the information in your graphic organizer to fill in the writing frame.

The ocean has three zones, or layers. The top layer is called the

_____. This layer _____

_____.

Many animals, such as _____

_____ swim here.

The middle layer is called the _____.

This layer _____

_____. A few animals,

such as _____ live here.

The bottom layer is called the _____.

This layer _____.

Very, very few animals, such as _____

_____ live here.

Use the writing frame above as a model to write a description of the layers in the Earth. Look in your science textbook if you need facts that will help you fill in the frame.

Text Feature

Special Type

Take a look at a page of nonfiction and what do you see? All kinds of **special type**! There are headings, **boldfaced** words, words in *italics*, words in parentheses ( ), and words in different **fonts**, different sizes, and even different colors. Why? Words in special type stand out. They seem to say, "Pay attention to us!" Use these clues to help you remember the ideas in the text.

Step 1 **The title is usually big. It announces what the article is about.** This article is about pets that are a problem.

Step 2 **The headings stand out. Don't skip them! They tell you what the next part of the article will be about.** The first heading, Too Big to Handle, tells you that the paragraph will be about pets that get too big.

Step 3 **Important vocabulary about the topic may be bold, underlined, or *italic*.** The important vocabulary in this article is boldfaced. Some of these words may be new to you. Be sure you understand what they mean.

Step 4 **A word in parentheses (puh-REN-thuh-seez) tells you how to pronounce, or say, the word before it.** The article shows how to pronounce the word *boa*. You may be surprised that it has two syllables.

Practice Your Skills!

1. Underline the headings.

2. Circle the boldfaced words.

3. Why does the writer want you to pay attention to the headings and boldfaced words?

PAIR SHARE What three important ideas do the title and headings tell you?

Problem Pets

Lizards, frogs, and snakes can be great pets. But some of these animals are destroying wildlife in Florida.

Too Big to Handle

Thousands of baby Nile monitor lizards, Cuban tree frogs, and boa (BOH-uh) constrictors are shipped to the U.S. each year. They are sold as pets. But as they grow up, they become large and hard to handle.

Nile monitor lizards, for example, grow to more than five feet long. When the lizards stop being fun little pets, their owners **release** them, or set them free. In the wild, the lizards eat the eggs of an owl that is **endangered**. The Cuban tree frogs and boa constrictors are also snacking on many of Florida's native lizards and birds.

Think Before Buying

Dumping these pets in the wild is **illegal**, or against the law, but it is hard to catch people doing it. The best solution is for people to think twice before buying a wild animal as a pet.

Nile monitor lizards are excellent swimmers and usually live near riverbanks. They often hide in holes that are dug by other animals.

Practice Your Skills!

Before You Read

Preview the article. Check (✔) the special features it has.

_____ boldfaced words
_____ headings
_____ chart
_____ map
_____ pronunciations

As You Read

• Did you read the title and headings?
❑ Yes ❑ No

• Did you figure out how to pronounce _salvinia?_
❑ Yes ❑ No

• Did you figure out what _habitats_ means?
❑ Yes ❑ No

• Explain how you used the special type.

After You Read

1. Why does the article call the snake, fish, and weevil "aliens"?

2. How is the effect of the weevil different from the other two animals?

PAIR SHARE What are some ways that animals might get to new habitats?

Animal Invaders

Alien creatures are invading all the time—but not from outer space. They are animal species (SPEE-sheez) that move from one part of the world to another. A new animal in a new place can mean big trouble for native plants and animals. Here are a few animal invaders that traveled from their **habitats**, or natural homes, to other places.

Brown Tree Snake

The **brown tree snake** is native to New Guinea, the Solomon Islands, and parts of Australia. About 50 years ago, these snakes arrived on the island of Guam. They were probably on a ship. They ate nearly all of Guam's **native** forest birds. The brown tree snakes also crawl onto the island's power lines and damage them.

Snakehead Fish

The **snakehead fish** is native to Southeast Asia. One summer, it somehow turned up in Maryland. This air-breathing fish species has a mouthful of sharp teeth. It is even able to move across land! It eats other fish, tadpoles, and even small ducks. The fish that was found in Maryland ate all the native life forms it could find.

Weevil

Some invader species are a solution to a problem! The **weevil** is a bug from Australia. Recently, scientists brought it to Louisiana to kill _another_ invader species—a plant from Brazil called giant salvinia (sal-VIN-ee-uh). This plant has killed many native plants in Louisiana. The weevil eats only giant salvinia. As long as the weevil doesn't start eating anything else, it could be a great help!

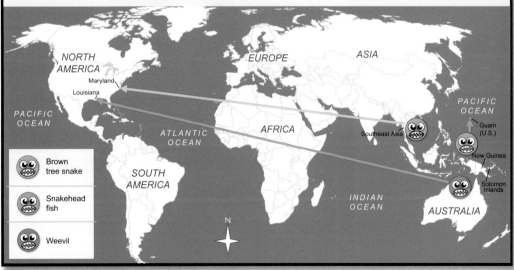

On Your Own

Read the article. Complete the four boxes. Write what each kind of special type tells you.

Title

It tells

Pronunciation

It tells

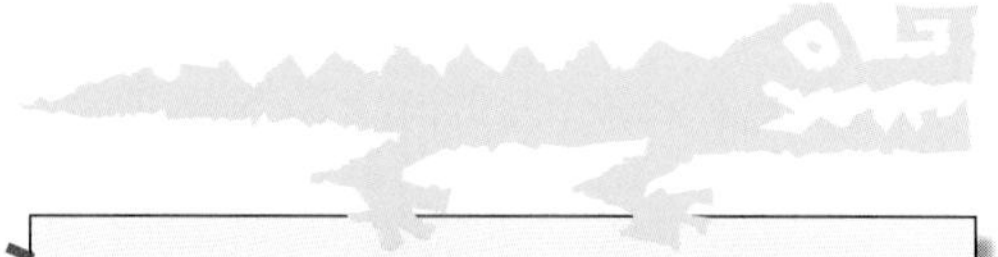

Reptile Facts

Reptiles include turtles, lizards, snakes, and crocodiles. They are all **vertebrates** (VUR-tuh-brayts), animals with backbones.

Temperature

All reptiles are cold-blooded, so that the temperature of their bodies is the same as the air around them. Reptiles make sure that they never get too hot or too cold. There are reptiles everywhere on Earth, except in Antarctica.

Food

Most reptiles are **carnivores** and feed on any animals they can catch. Reptiles have long, sticky tongues for trapping the insects they eat. Some snakes have a poisonous bite, as well, which they use to kill their **prey** (pray).

Heading

It tells

Boldfaced Word

It tells

Special Type

You may see a colorful title, headings at the beginning of each section, **boldfaced words**, words in *italics,* and pronunciations (proh-nun-see-AY-shunz) inside parentheses. Each kind of special type is a clue to help you figure out the important words and ideas in the text. First you must know how to use them.

Step 1 **You can't miss the title. It's usually big. It tells you what the article is about.** The article below is about holiday celebrations.

Step 2 **The headings stand out. They tell you what you will read about in the next part of the article.** The heading tells you the name of the holiday you will read about.

Step 3 **Important vocabulary about the topic may be bold, underlined, or *italic.*** The word **tradition** is in dark type so that you notice it. Make sure you know what it means.

Step 4 **A word in parentheses tells you how to pronounce, or say, the word before it.** You may not know how to say piñata, because it's in another language. The pronunciation helps you.

Practice Your Skills!

1. Circle the boldfaced word that means "a big dinner."

2. Underline under the pronunciation of *piñata.*

3. Does this sentence belong in this article? "Families light candles for Kwanzaa." Why or why not?

PAIR SHARE What two other headings would you add to "Holiday Celebrations"?

HOLIDAY CELEBRATIONS

LAS POSADAS
DECEMBER 22–29

My family celebrates Las Posadas (lahz poh-SAH-dahz) for nine days before Christmas each year. It's my family's **tradition** to have a big dinner on the ninth night of Las Posadas. We do it every year. My grandparents and all my aunts, uncles, and cousins come to our house for a **feast** with lots of different foods. We hang a piñata (peen-YAH-tuh). After dinner, all the kids try to break it. The best part is when the piñata finally breaks. I love the treats that fall out!

Before You Read

Preview the article. Check (✔) the special features it has.

_____ boldfaced words
_____ headings
_____ photos
_____ graph
_____ map

As You Read

- Did you use the title and headings to figure out what you were going to read?
  ❏ Yes   ❏ No

- Did you pay attention to the boldfaced words?
  ❏ Yes   ❏ No

- Did you figure out how to pronounce *myth?*
  ❏ Yes   ❏ No

- Explain how you used the special type.

After You Read

1. How is Thanksgiving today like Thanksgiving in 1621? How is it different?

2. What special type was used in the article? Why?

PAIR SHARE Before reading, did you think any of the myths were true? If so, which ones?

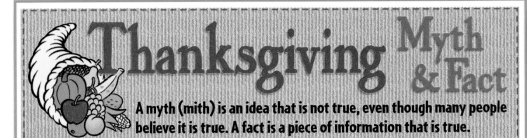

Thanksgiving Myth & Fact

A myth (mith) is an idea that is not true, even though many people believe it is true. A fact is a piece of information that is true.

Myth The Pilgrims wore somber (SAHM-bur) clothes. They were dark and dull.

Fact The Pilgrims wore different colors. Their clothes were red, yellow, blue, and purple. And they did not have buckles on their shoes.

Myth The first Thanksgiving **celebration** in 1621 lasted one day. The Pilgrims and Wampanoag (WAM-puh-NOH-ag) Indians ate a feast that included cranberry sauce, mashed potatoes, and apple pie.

Fact The first Thanksgiving celebration lasted almost a week. It was called a harvest feast. The Pilgrims and Indians ate turkey, deer meat, mashed pumpkin, and seafood.

Myth The first Thanksgiving was a quiet time of thanks and prayer. The Pilgrims were very serious.

Fact The feast was a time of games and celebration. People played a game called "Pitching the Bar." Players took turns tossing a log to see who could throw it the farthest.

More Myths and Facts

- The Pilgrims did not call themselves "Pilgrims." They called themselves "English" because they were from England.
- The Pilgrims built their village on what had once been a home site of the Wampanoag people.

On Your Own

Read the article. Then in each box, write what the word in special type is called. Use these labels: **pronunciation**, **heading**, **title**, **boldfaced word**. Also tell the purpose of the special type.

VISIT THE PAST

A PILGRIM VILLAGE

Each year, many people visit a Pilgrim village in Plymouth, Massachusetts. It is a museum called Plimoth Plantation, a **re-creation** of the town built by the Pilgrims. Live actors dress as Pilgrims and show visitors what life was like in 1627. You might see women grinding corn, taking care of the animals, and cooking on the hearth (hahrth), the floor of a fireplace. The men might be fixing one of the wooden buildings or working in the cornfields.

ACTING A PART

Each actor in the village has taken on the name and life history of a real person who lived in the village in 1627. They have to stay in character. That means they have to **pretend**, or make believe, they are living in 1627. They have to act as if they don't know anything that happened after 1627. So, remember, if you ask a question like, "Do you have a television set?" they won't know what you're talking about! No one in 1627 ever heard of a television set!

What is it?

What's its purpose?

What is it?

What's its purpose?

What is it?

What's its purpose?

1. What does *pretend* mean?
2. Which word rhymes with the name *Garth?*
3. Under which heading would this sentence belong? *The village has homes, gardens, and animal pens.*

Cause/Effect

Practice Your Skills!

Before You Read

Vocabulary Read the word pairs. Then check the column that shows the connection between the two words.

WHAT'S THE CONNECTION?

	Synonym	Antonym
destroy ruin		
prepared unprepared		
calm upset		
patience impatience		
damage harm		

As You Read

Text Structure This article tells what a tornado causes a family to do. It also tells the effects of a tornado. To find the cause of what the family did, ask yourself, "Why did they do that?" To find the effects of the tornado, ask yourself, "What happened because of the tornado?"

Text Feature How does the special type help you understand the article?

After You Read

1. Why was the supply closet a good place to be?

2. Why did the family keep candles in the supply closet?

3. What other jobs can be as dangerous as a storm chaser's job?

IT'S TORNADO

Every year from April to June, the central part of the United States is hit by dozens of tornadoes. Meet a kid who lived through one of these powerful storms!

Safe From the Storm

One evening last June, 8-year-old Jackie and her parents saw a **tornado** (tor-NAY-doh) headed toward their house. They knew the terrible effects of a tornado. It could destroy houses, flip cars over, and rip trees from the ground. But the family stayed safe because they were well prepared and remained calm.

The Storm Moves In

Jackie, her parents, and her older brother live in Buffalo Lake, a town in Minnesota (min-uh-SOH-tuh). They learned from a TV news report that the tornado was coming. "Then my dad told me he saw the tornado through the window," says Jackie. "So, we went downstairs to the basement and looked through a window. It was the first time I ever saw a tornado!"

In the basement, the family went into a supply closet. This would **protect** them and kept them safe from flying glass if the windows of the house got smashed in. Suddenly, all the electricity went out. But the family had candles ready.

They could hear the storm outside. "I heard trees falling down," says Jackie. After the storm passed, they walked up the stairs and saw that most of their house was gone. The tornado also caused much **damage** to the town. It smashed houses, stores, a post office, and a church. Therefore, there was a lot of work to be done.

Picking Up the Pieces

The family's house has been rebuilt since the tornado. And the buildings in the town have been fixed up. But most important, Jackie and her family were not hurt. Being prepared for a tornado kept them safe.

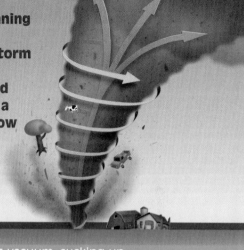

HOW TORNADOES WORK

A tornado is a spinning column of air that stretches from a storm cloud down to the ground. It is shaped like a funnel, with a wide top and narrow bottom. It forms during a giant thunderstorm called a supercell.

- A tornado acts like a vacuum, sucking up everything in its path.
- The winds of a tornado twist in a direction that is counterclockwise, or opposite to the way the hands of a clock move.
- The funnel of a tornado is called a vortex.

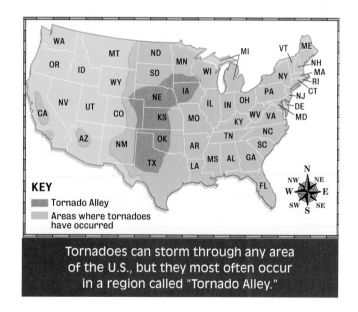

KEY

■ Tornado Alley
■ Areas where tornadoes have occurred

Tornadoes can storm through any area of the U.S., but they most often occur in a region called "Tornado Alley."

Cause/Effect

Reread "It's Tornado Time." Fill in the graphic organizer. First, read each **cause**. Then, write each **effect**.

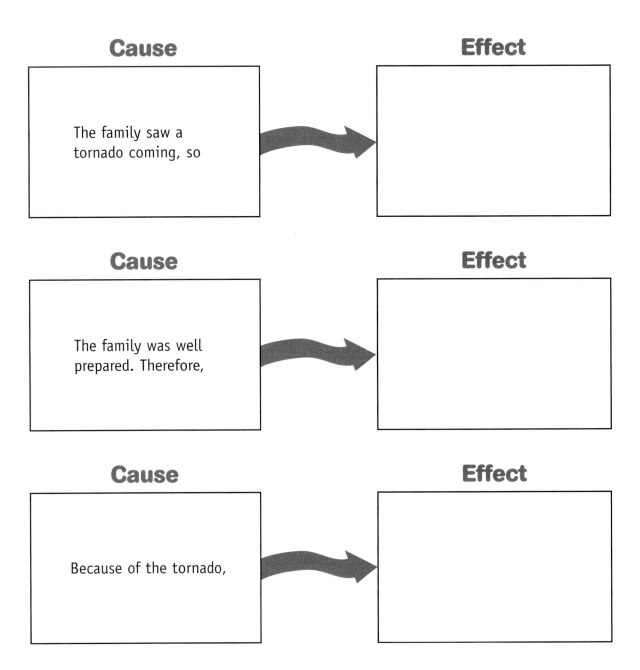

Cause

The family saw a tornado coming, so

Effect

Cause

The family was well prepared. Therefore,

Effect

Cause

Because of the tornado,

Effect

Retell Use the graphic organizer above to retell "It's Tornado Time" in your own words. Include as much information as you can remember. Look back at the article to help you with details you may have missed.

Writing Frame

Use the information in your graphic organizer to fill in the writing frame.

The family saw a tornado coming, so they _____

_____

_____

_____.

They were well prepared. Therefore, _____.

Because of the tornado, _____

_____.

and _____

_____

_____.

Afterward, the house was rebuilt and the town was fixed up.

 Use the writing frame above as a model to write about another cause and effect such as the tides, changes in matter, magnets, or other kinds of bad weather. Look in your science book if you need facts that will help you fill in the frame.

Text Feature

Flow Charts

Nonfiction may explain how something is made. Often, there is a diagram that shows each step in the process. The diagram is called a **flow chart**. It's important to follow the steps in the correct order. Otherwise, you might put the corn into boxes before it's made into flakes!

Step 1 **Read the title. It tells you what the flow chart is about.** The chart below shows how corn becomes corn flakes.

Step 2 **Follow the numbers. They tell you the order of the steps.** Always start at number 1. In this flow chart, arrows also point the way.

Step 3 **Look at the illustration for each step and read the caption.**

Step 4 **Make sure you understand what happens in each step.** Use the illustrations and captions to be sure you understand how corn is made into corn-flake cereal.

Practice Your Skills!

1. Underline the caption that tells what happens after the corn is toasted.

2. Circle the illustration that shows what happens last.

PAIR SHARE What are some steps you could add to the flow chart? Why do you think the flow chart doesn't show them?

From Corn to Cereal

1. Corn is sent from the farm to the factory.

2. The corn kernels are taken off the cobs and cooked. Then, the cooked corn is dried out.

3. Next, large rollers squeeze the corn flat into flakes. After that, the corn flakes are toasted in ovens.

4. The corn flakes are put into bags and then boxes.

5. Trucks take the boxes to stores.

Before You Read

Preview the article. Check (✔) the special features it has.

_____ flow chart
_____ caption
_____ map
_____ illustration
_____ time line

As You Read

• Did you follow the numbers and arrows in order?
❏ Yes ❏ No

• Did you study the drawings and read the captions?
❏ Yes ❏ No

• Did you connect the information in the article with the flow chart?
❏ Yes ❏ No

• Explain how you read the flow chart.

After You Read

1. What did you already know about the topic? What did you learn?

2. Why did the writer include the flow chart?

 PAIR SHARE Why is the flow chart a circle?

A Farmer's Year

Most of the food we eat is grown on farms. Your oranges may have been grown in California. The corn that your cereal is made of may have come from a farm in Iowa. Your pizza dough may be made from wheat grown in Kansas.

A farmer's year is a busy one. It is organized around planting, growing, and harvesting crops. Although a farmer works long hours to grow crops, technology makes farming easier than it was in the past. Machines are used to plow, plant, and spread **fertilizer**, chemicals that help plants grow. A **combine**, a machine that harvests grain such as wheat, does the job quickly. For example, it cuts the wheat and separates the grain from the stalks.

The flow chart shows the different jobs a farmer does throughout the year. In different places around the world, these steps happen at different times depending on the seasons.

How Crops Are Grown

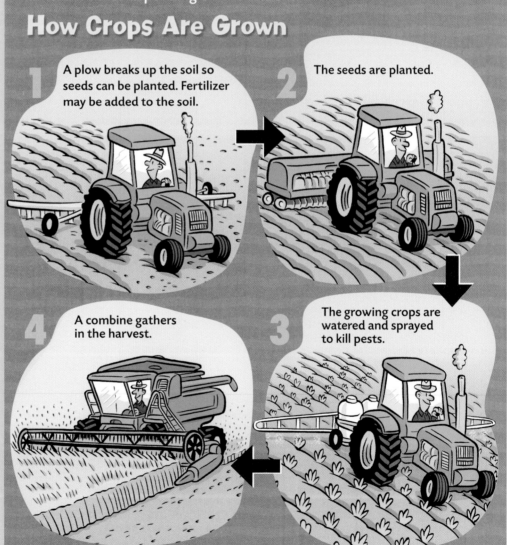

1 A plow breaks up the soil so seeds can be planted. Fertilizer may be added to the soil.

2 The seeds are planted.

3 The growing crops are watered and sprayed to kill pests.

4 A combine gathers in the harvest.

On Your Own

Imagine your favorite kind of sandwich. How do you make it? Picture the steps in your mind. Then, make a flow chart to show each step in order.

- Write the title, such as **How to Make a _____ Sandwich.**

- On scrap paper, write out the steps as you think of them. Then, number the steps in the right order. You will use these steps for your flow chart.

- Start at box number 1. Look at your list and write what you do first. Then go to box number 2, and write what you do next.

How to Make a _____ Sandwich

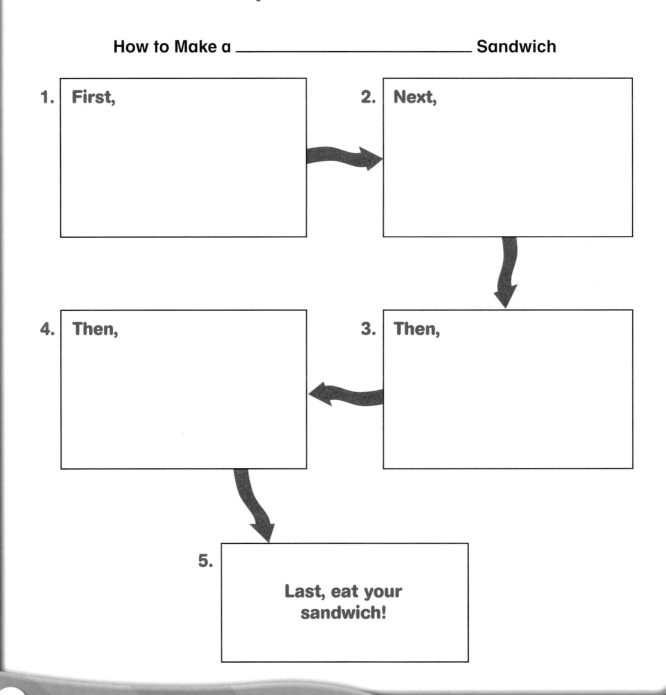

1. **First,**

2. **Next,**

4. **Then,**

3. **Then,**

5. **Last, eat your sandwich!**

Flow Charts

In science, you read about all kinds of cycles—the life cycle of an animal, the cycles of the moon, the cycle of seasons. A cycle can be pictured in a **flow chart**. A flow chart is a kind of diagram that shows the steps in which something happens. Each step is shown in the order it happens. Some flow charts go around and around in a circle. That's because they show a cycle that never ends. Follow the steps to read the flow chart.

Step 1 **Read the title. It tells you what the flow chart is about.** The chart below shows how evergreen cones make seeds.

Step 2 **Follow the numbers and the arrows. They show the order of the steps.** Always start at number 1.

Step 3 **Look at the illustration and read the caption.** They give you information about each step in the life cycle of an evergreen cone.

Step 4 **Make sure you understand what happens in each step.** Use the illustrations and captions to be sure you understand how an evergreen makes seeds that grow into new plants.

Practice Your Skills!

1. Circle the things that will grow into new plants.

2. Draw your own picture for step 5.

PAIR SHARE Why is there an arrow from step 5 to step 1?

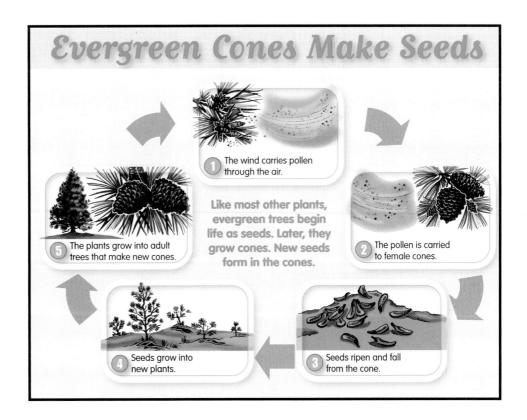

Evergreen Cones Make Seeds

1. The wind carries pollen through the air.

2. The pollen is carried to female cones.

3. Seeds ripen and fall from the cone.

4. Seeds grow into new plants.

5. The plants grow into adult trees that make new cones.

Like most other plants, evergreen trees begin life as seeds. Later, they grow cones. New seeds form in the cones.

Practice Your Skills!

Before You Read

Preview the article. Check (✔) the special features it has.

_____ title
_____ pronunciations
_____ labels
_____ time line
_____ map
_____ flow chart

As You Read

- Did you read the title of the flow chart?
  ❏ Yes ❏ No

- What did you follow on the flow chart?
  ❏ numbers
  ❏ arrows

- Did you look at each step in order?
  ❏ Yes ❏ No

- Explain how you read the flow chart.

After You Read

1. Would a plant be in the middle of a food chain? Explain.

2. Are you a producer or a consumer?

3. Where are you in a food chain?

PAIR SHARE How is this flow chart different from the one about evergreen cones? How is it the same?

What Is a Food Chain?

All living things need energy from food. Plants make their own food. That's something that neither you nor any other animal can do. So where do animals get their food?

Look at the flow chart below. Every arrow goes from one organism to another—from what is eaten to what it eats. This is called a **food chain**. A food chain is a series of organisms that depend on each other for food.

A food chain can be very long, but most food chains start with plants. Plants are **producers** (pruh-DEW-serz). Plants use air, water, and energy from sunlight to produce, or make, food. An animal then eats the plant. The animals that eat producers are called **consumers** (kuhn-SOO-merz). You can see on the flow chart that some consumers eat other consumers, too.

How a Food Chain Works

A plant uses energy from sunlight to make food.

An insect eats the plant. The insect then gets the energy of the plant.

A mouse eats the insect. The mouse then gets the energy of the insect and the plant.

A hawk eats the snake. The hawk then gets the energy of the snake, mouse, insect, and plant.

A snake eats the mouse. The snake then gets the energy of the mouse, the insect, and the plant.

On Your Own

Make a flow chart that shows how a person fits into the food chain.

Food Chain
Producer

First: Imagine a kid who drank milk this morning. That's the consumer in box 3.

1

Next: What animal did that milk come from?

_____

Go to box 2. Draw that animal.

_____

Animal That Ate the Producer

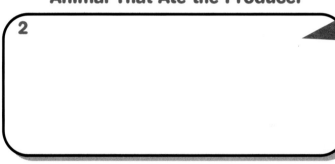

2

Then: What food did that animal eat?

_____

Go to box 1. Draw the animal eating the food. That food is the first organism in the food chain—the producer.

_____

Consumer

Last: Write a caption under each picture. Tell what the picture shows.

3

_____

Talk with a partner to answer the questions below. What is the plant eater in this flow chart? You are last in any of the food chains you're in. Why is that?

Sequence

Practice Your Skills!

Before You Read

Vocabulary Write each vocabulary word next to its synonym on the chart.

harvest   factory
ground   consumer

Word	Synonym
crushed	
gather	
soil	
buyer	
plant	

As You Read

Text Structure The article tells the steps in making peanut butter. Look for clue words such as *first, next, then, finally,* and *last.* They will help you follow the sequence, or the order of the steps. Circle these words in the article.

Text Feature How does the flow chart help you understand and remember the information?

After You Read

1. If you could add a box to the flow chart, what would it be? Why?

2. The article explains two sequences. What are they?

3. How has the writer made it easy for you to find information?

FROM PEANUTS to PEANUT BUTTER

You just got home from school and you're so-o-o hungry! What can you make that's quick and easy, good for you, and tasty? If you're like most kids, you would say, "A peanut butter and jelly sandwich!" Have you ever wondered how peanut butter is made?

ON THE FARM

You probably already know that peanut butter is made from peanuts. But did you know that peanuts are really seeds? Farmers plant shelled peanuts in April. The peanuts grow into leafy bushes about two feet tall.

The peanut plant is unusual. After the plant flowers, the stalks, or branches, bend over and push back into the ground. And that's where the plant's fruit, the new peanuts, grow—under the ground!

Fall is the time to **harvest**. First, the farmer plows the peanuts out of the ground with a tractor. Next, the plants are allowed to dry in the sun for a few days. Then, the farmer drives a combine (KOM-bine) over the plants. After that, the **machine** separates the plants from the peanuts and dumps the peanuts into a trailer truck.

Finally, the peanuts are sold. They can be made into many products, such as peanut butter or peanut oil.

AT THE FACTORY

The peanuts that will be made into peanut butter travel to a **factory**, or plant, where peanut butter is made.

HOW PEANUT BUTTER IS MADE

1. After the peanuts are harvested in the fall, they go to a peanut butter factory.

2. The shells are taken off the peanuts.

3. The peanuts are roasted in ovens. Their skins are removed.

4. Machines grind the peanuts into peanut butter. Then the peanut butter is poured into jars.

5. The jars are sent all over the world, some by truck, others by ship.

TO STORES

Jars of peanut butter are sold in neighborhood stores, where **consumers** like you and your family can buy them. And all those things had to happen to make the peanut butter for your sandwich!

Fun Facts

- It takes about 850 peanuts to make a jar of peanut butter!

- Americans eat about 10 billion peanut butter and jelly sandwiches in a year!

- More people like creamy peanut butter than the crunchy kind.

- Georgia is the state that grows the most peanuts.

- Two peanut farmers have been U.S. Presidents—Thomas Jefferson and Jimmy Carter.

Sequence

Reread "From Peanuts to Peanut Butter." Then finish the graphic organizer to show the sequence of how peanuts grow on the farm. Fill in the steps in the order they happen. Add drawings if you would like to.

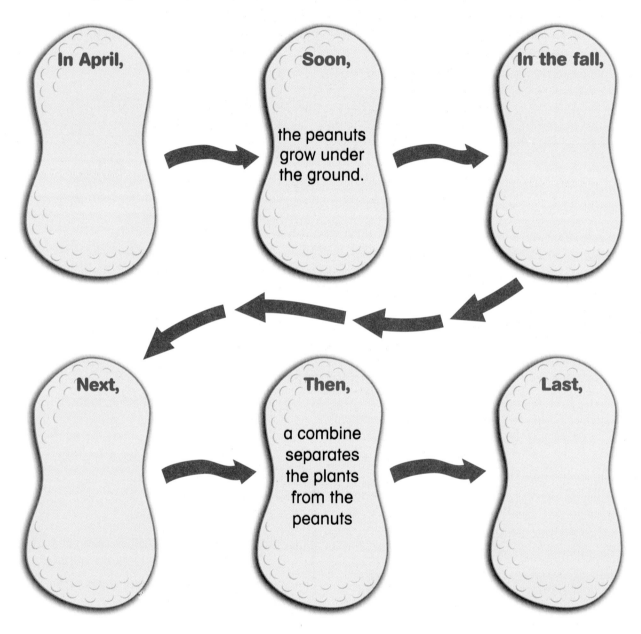

In April,

Soon, the peanuts grow under the ground.

In the fall,

Next,

Then, a combine separates the plants from the peanuts

Last,

 Retell

Use the flow chart above to retell the section On the Farm in your own words. Include as much information as you can remember. Look back at the article to help you with details you may have missed.

Writing Frame

Use the information in your graphic organizer to fill in the writing frame.

This is how peanuts grow. In April, _____

_____.

Then, in the fall, _____

_____.

Next, the plants have to _____.

After that, _____

_____

_____.

and _____

_____

_____.

Last, the peanuts are sold.

 Use the writing frame above as a model to write about another sequence, such as how corn or wheat is grown. Or how a food such as pasta is made. Look in your social studies textbook if you need facts that will help you fill in the frame.

Text Feature

Headings

Science textbooks and magazine articles present information in a way that highlights the main idea and details in the article. Writers of these books and magazines want their readers to "get it." So, they put in clues to help them.

- The **title** tells what the article is about. This is the topic of the *whole* article.

- **Headings** give information related to the main ideas. These are the main ideas for each section of the text. Headings often are shown in some special kind of type, such as in all CAPITAL LETTERS, a different color, or **boldfaced**.

- **Details** are the facts about each main idea in the text. Under each heading, you will find text containing these details.

Practice Your Skills!

1. Put an **X** on the article's title.

2. Circle the headings in the article to learn the main ideas.

3. Underline one important detail under each heading.

PAIR SHARE Why are zoos important places for animals and people?

New Animal Babies
NEW HOPE FOR THE ENDANGERED

Six Bengal white tiger cubs and a baby bonobo (boh-NO-boh), which is a kind of small chimpanzee, were born at zoos recently. Both species are endangered. Each birth means the species has a better chance to survive.

North America
U.S.
Cincinnati Zoo
Atlantic Ocean
Pacific Ocean
South America
Buenos Aires Zoo
ARGENTINA

Baby Bonobo

Vijay (VEE-jay), a male bonobo, was born at the Cincinnati Zoo. Vijay's mother had trouble caring for him, so zoo workers have been feeding and playing with him.

Vijay is one of about 150 bonobos living in zoos. About 5,000 bonobos are left in the wild. They are found in the rain forests of the Democratic Republic of Congo, in Africa. Bonobos are endangered because people hunt them and cut down forests they need to survive.

Tigers' Tale

Bengal white tigers, found in Asia, are also dying out because they are hunted. Six Bengal white tiger cubs raise the number of white tigers in the world—to just 210.

The cubs were born at the Buenos Aires Zoo, in Argentina. Like Vijay, the cubs are cared for by zoo workers.

Practice Your Skills!

Before You Read

Preview the article. Check (✔) the special features it has.

_____ title
_____ caption
_____ headings
_____ graph
_____ photo
_____ pronunciations

As You Read

• Did you read the title of the article?
❑ Yes ❑ No

• Did you read the headings to learn the main ideas?
❑ Yes ❑ No

• Did you read the boldfaced words and think about their meanings?
❑ Yes ❑ No

• Explain the steps you followed to read the article.

After You Read

1. What is the main idea of this article?

2. What information did you learn from the headings? How did they help you read and understand the article?

PAIR SHARE What did you learn from the article that surprised you? Why?

Trunk Talk

What Is Communication?

If you want to make new school friends or tell your teacher something, you need to **communicate**, or share information, ideas, or feelings. Communication is just as important for African elephants. Scientists have learned that these animals communicate as much as we do.

How Do Elephants Communicate?

Like humans, elephants give facts and show their feelings to each other. Instead of using words, the elephants use their bodies and make sounds.

African elephants make about 70 different sounds. They rumble, squeal, and cry to say things like, "I'm over here," "Let's go," and "Hello."

They also use their faces to **express**, or show, how they feel. If they are scared, they widen their eyes. If they are excited to see other elephants they raise their ears. If they are playing happily, they often smile!

The scientists are making a list of elephant signals and sounds. Since little is known about these amazing animals, the list will help people understand them better.

On Your Own

Below is an article about animal communication. Follow the directions:

- Circle the headings.
- Read the article.
- Underline one detail in each paragraph.

HOW DO ANIMALS COMMUNICATE?

Communication is one way animals survive in their habitats. Animals communicate, or "talk" to each other, to warn off enemies, mark their territory so other animals will stay away, identify themselves, or find and attract mates. There are four unique ways animals communicate.

By Sight

Some animals have a special color or shape that helps them to communicate to other animals. For example, a male deer with large antlers is telling other deer that it is stronger and more powerful than them. The bright feathers of a male bird tell how healthy it is to possible mates.

By Hearing

Most animals make sounds to talk to each other. These range from the roar of an angry lion to the distressed song of an injured whale. Dolphins even use sound to find food!

By Touch

Animals also use touch to express their feelings or needs. For example, when a cat rubs up against you, it is trying to talk to you. What might it be saying?

By Smell

Some animals use odor or saliva to communicate. For example, when a skunk sprays its horrible smell, it is telling its enemies to stay away. Gross!

Write three questions about the article. Ask partners to answer the questions.

1. _____

2. _____

3. _____

Text Feature

Headings

When you read nonfiction, you need to know *What's this article about? What's the main idea?* Writers of nonfiction give you clues to help you answer those questions.

Step 1 **Read the title to find out what the article is about.** The title tells us that this article explains reasons why communities change over time.

Step 2 **Read the headings to find out the main ideas.** The headings tell us that we will learn three reasons why communities change.

Step 3 **Look for details to get more facts.** Under each heading are facts about the main idea.

Practice Your Skills!

1. Put an **X** on the article's title.

2. Circle the headings in the article to learn the main ideas.

3. What invention helped Houston grow? How?

PAIR SHARE Which of these reasons has caused your community to change? Why else might a community change?

Why Do Communities Change?

Houston, Texas, is a very hot and humid city. It is difficult to live and work in a place that hot! Therefore, this city grew very fast when air conditioning was invented. Here's three ways cities grow.

① Jobs

Long ago, people grew or made the things they needed. For example, farmers raised sheep. They would cut the wool and make clothing from it. If a farmer needed to make a table, he might cut down a tree, saw the wood, and build it himself. Today, people don't make all the things they need. Instead, they work at jobs to earn money to buy the things they need.

② Transportation

Highways built next to communities help businesses grow. People traveling along the highway find it easy to stop to buy things. As more people come to an area, the towns and cities grow larger. This may even result in more roads being built. People can then get around their communities faster and with greater ease.

③ Inventions and Technology

Technology and new ideas have changed the way we live, work, and communicate. Long ago, if you wanted to speak to someone, you had to write a letter or travel long distances by horse to see the person. Today, cellular phones and other inventions make communication easier. We can talk to someone halfway around the world in an instant!

Before You Read

Preview the article. Check (✔) the special features it has.

____ introduction
____ headings
____ graph
____ captions
____ map

As You Read

• Did you read the title of the article?
❏ Yes ❏ No

• Did you read the headings to learn the main ideas?
❏ Yes ❏ No

• Did you read the captions?
❏ Yes ❏ No

• Explain the steps you followed to read the article.

After You Read

1. What is the main idea of this article?

2. What information did you learn from the headings? How did they help you read and understand the article?

PAIR SHARE Why is the Mississippi River so important to the U.S.?

The Mighty Mississippi River

The Mississippi River was an important water highway long before roads.

River Uses

Native Americans used the Mississippi River for travel and trade. Today the river is used the same way. Factories and farms use the river to ship goods for trade to other parts of the United States and around the world. Riverboats also carry passengers from place to place.

Parts of a River

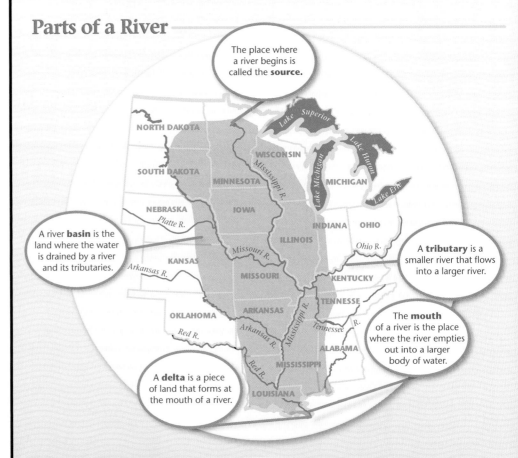

The place where a river begins is called the **source**.

A river **basin** is the land where the water is drained by a river and its tributaries.

A **tributary** is a smaller river that flows into a larger river.

The **mouth** of a river is the place where the river empties out into a larger body of water.

A **delta** is a piece of land that forms at the mouth of a river.

Views of a River

A view of the Mississippi River Delta from space.

Cargo ships and other boats travel along the Mississippi River.

On Your Own

Read the article below. Then use the information to complete the outline.

The Ohio River

The Ohio River begins in Pittsburgh, Pennsylvania, and flows 981 miles to join the Mississippi River in Cairo, Illinois. This river has been important for traveling and trade throughout the history of the United States.

Settlers Move West

After the American Revolutionary War, many people traveled west on the Ohio River. They used flatboats to make the long trip. People had to steer the boats by hand. This was difficult. And, the boats only went one way since the settlers broke them apart and used the wood to build their homes. However, everything changed in 1811 when the first steamboat was made. Steamboats made it possible to travel faster and easier. Travel and trade on the rivers increased.

Improving the River

Still, travel on the river was difficult. Shifting sandbars, snags, rocks, and the ever-changing river depths made river travel dangerous. The people using the river asked the U.S. government to step in and improve the river. They did. The U.S. government paid for the sand bars to be cleared away. They also set up a system of dams to keep the water at the same level all the time. This helped the river become a safe way for travel.

Increasing Trade

With these improvements, boats carrying people and goods increased. Now, 150 million tons of goods are shipped up and down the river every year. The Ohio River continues to be an important source of travel and trade for the people living along its shores and beyond.

Topic: _____

Main Idea: _____

_____

Details: 1. _____

2. _____

3. _____

Text Structure

Sequence

Sea Turtles on

Practice
Your Skills!

Before You Read

Vocabulary Here are some important words from the article. Think about their definitions. Then answer the questions.

migrate   marine
odor   creature

Where does a <u>marine</u> animal live?

What <u>creatures</u> can you find in the sea?

What animals <u>migrate</u> each year?

What has a nice <u>odor</u>?

As You Read

Text Structure This article details the migration of sea turtles. As you read, look for sequence words such as *then, next, finally,* and *during*. Circle these words.

Text Feature How do the headings help you organize your thinking as you read the article?

After You Read

1. How do sea turtles know where to swim?

2. How did scientists learn about sea turtle migration?

3. What information in the article surprised you? Why?

From Brazil to Ascension Island

Get a whiff of this! Green sea turtles that migrate from Brazil to Ascension (ah-SEN-shun) Island travel about 1,350 miles. How do they do it? With a little help from their noses!

The Nose Knows

When the turtles begin their **voyage**, or journey, to Ascension Island, they already know in which direction to swim. But as they approach the island, they need a little help. That's when the wind and the turtle's sense of smell play an important role.

As the wind blows, it carries odors from the island. These odors reach migrating turtles many miles away. When the turtles smell the odors, they know the island is near and can find their way there.

Testing Turtles

Scientists have always **suspected**, or guessed, that the sense of smell helps these turtles migrate. Recently they proved it with an experiment.

During the experiment, the scientists placed six turtles in different parts of the ocean. Three of the turtles were placed in an area where the wind blew odors from the island in their direction. These turtles found the island in just a few days.

The other three turtles were placed in an area where the wind blew odors up and away from them. These turtles couldn't smell the odors, so it took them up to a month to find the island. One of the turtles even gave up and headed back to Brazil! Scientists have been studying green sea turtles for many years. They are excited to finally discover the secret behind the turtles' successful migration to Ascension Island.

Turtle Truths

🐢 Green sea turtles can lay about 115 eggs at one time.

🐢 Most young sea turtles eat jellyfish, snails, oysters, and other marine creatures. Adult green sea turtles, however, eat only plants.

🐢 Green sea turtles can be found in more regions that any other species of sea turtle. They live in tropical waters near the coasts of 139 countries.

the Move

Returning to a Place to Lay Her Eggs

1

This green sea turtle spends most of her life in the water. Now the sea turtle is on her way to the shore. She has an important job to do once she reaches land.

2

After traveling for days, the sea turtle reaches land. She has come to lay her eggs. It takes a lot of energy for her to pull herself onto the beach.

3

The sea turtle slowly drags her heavy body across the sand. While her **flippers** are excellent for swimming, they are not helpful for walking. She crawls until she finds a spot to make her nest.

4
A sea turtle's nest is a deep hole in the sand. To make the nest, the sea turtle uses her front flippers to push away sand. Then she uses her back flippers to dig a deep hole for her eggs.

5

The sea turtle lays one or two eggs at a time in the nest. She lays over 100 rubbery eggs in all. After she lays her eggs, she pushes sand over the nest. She hides her eggs from **predators**.

6

The **hatchlings**, or baby turtles, race to the water before hungry crabs and birds can eat them. When they reach the sea, hatchlings swim for days to find deep water. Then, the young turtles join many other sea creatures and settle into underwater life.

Sequence

Reread "Sea Turtles on the Move." Fill in the graphic organizer to show the steps a mother sea turtle takes to lay her eggs.

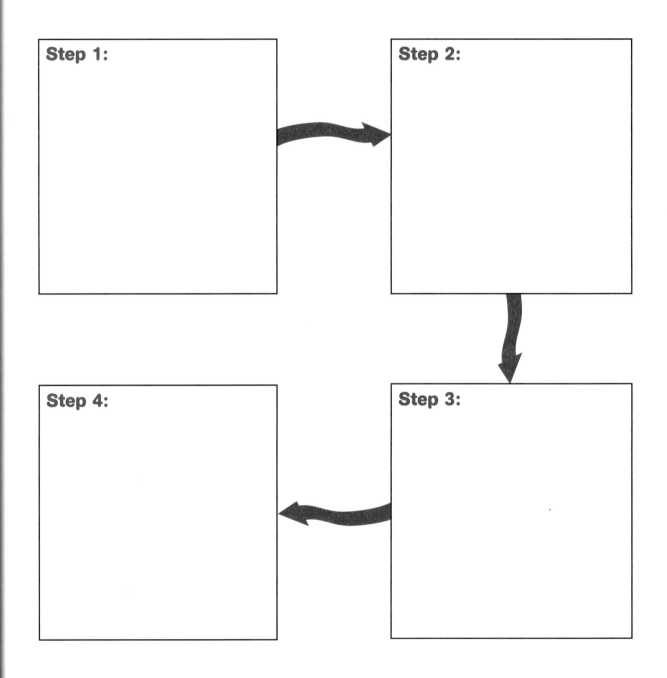

Step 1:

Step 2:

Step 4:

Step 3:

 Use the graphic organizer above to retell "Sea Turtles on the Move" in your own words. Remember to include each step a sea turtle takes to lay her eggs.

Writing Frame

Use the information in your graphic organizer to fill in the writing frame.

A green sea turtle must return to a place to lay her eggs.

First, _____

_____

_____ .

Then, _____

_____

_____ .

Next, _____

_____ .

After that, _____

_____ .

Finally, the baby turtles, called hatchlings, hatch and find their way to the

sea to swim with the other sea turtles.

 Use the writing frame above as a model to show the life cycle of another animal. Look in your science textbook if you need facts that will help you fill in the frame.

Graphs

A **pictograph**, sometimes called a picture graph, uses pictures to show how many there are of something. A pictograph always has a **key** that tells you what each picture stands for. Follow the steps to get the picture.

Step 1 **Read the title to find out what the graph shows.** The graph on this page shows how much trash one person threw away in a year.

Step 2 **Look at the labels for each row.** The labels on this graph tell you the kinds of trash.

Step 3 **Look at the key to find out the amount each symbol stands for.** Each picture of a garbage bag stands for 10 pounds of trash.

Step 4 **Count the number of pictures in each row. Then figure out the total number shown in each row.** Since each garbage bag stands for 10 pounds of trash, 2 garbage bags stand for 20 pounds, 3 garbage bags stand for 30 pounds, and so on.

Step 5 **Compare and contrast the information on the graph.** For example, what was the greatest amount of trash? How many pounds was it? What was the least amount? How many pounds was it?

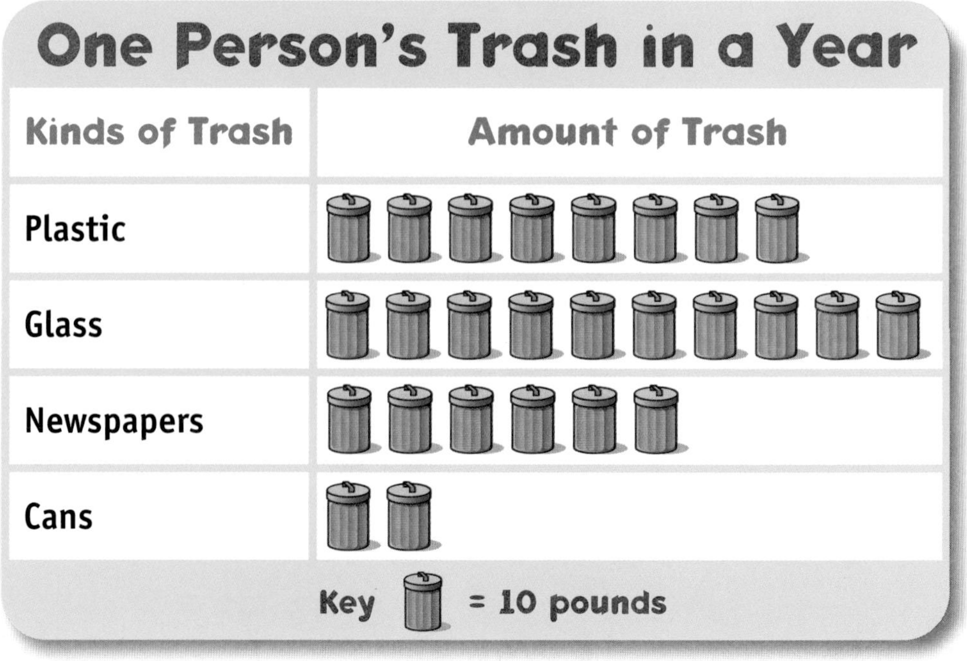

Practice Your Skills!

1. Put an **X** on the word that tells the period of time the graph shows.

2. Circle the word that names the largest amount of trash.

3. Did the person throw away more pounds of newspapers or plastic bottles?

PAIR SHARE How do these amounts compare with the trash you throw away?

One Person's Trash in a Year

Kinds of Trash	Amount of Trash
Plastic	🗑🗑🗑🗑🗑🗑🗑🗑
Glass	🗑🗑🗑🗑🗑🗑🗑🗑🗑🗑
Newspapers	🗑🗑🗑🗑🗑
Cans	🗑🗑

Key 🗑 = 10 pounds

Practice Your Skills!

Before You Read

Preview the article. Check (✔) the special features it has.

_____ headings
_____ caption
_____ illustration
_____ graph
_____ flow chart

As You Read

• Did you read the graph title and labels?
❏ Yes ❏ No

• What does the 💧 symbol stand for?
❏ ways to use water
❏ amount of water

• Circle all the ways the family used water.

• Explain how you read the pictograph.

After You Read

1. Which activity uses the least water?

2. Which uses more water—taking a shower or taking a bath?

PAIR SHARE How might this family save water?

Protect the Planet 🌍

Leaving on lights and electrical appliances when they're not needed is a waste of energy. Leaky faucets waste valuable water. Even throwing out your garbage without sorting it for recycling can cause problems for the environment. See how being wasteful in your home affects the world around you.

WATER

PROBLEM

We all need water to live, but there isn't always enough of it for everybody. Some areas have less water than others, and any area can have a water shortage. Each American uses about 183 gallons of fresh water every day! That's a lot of water, so wasting any of it is bad for people, plants, and animals.

HOW YOU CAN HELP

Turn off the water while you brush your teeth. You can also take shorter showers and fill the bathtub only halfway for a bath. Also, make sure your faucets aren't leaking.

A Family's Use of Water Every Day

Activity	Amount of Water Used
Drinking	💧
Taking a Shower	💧💧💧💧💧💧💧
Taking a Bath	💧💧💧💧💧💧💧💧💧
Brushing Teeth	💧
Washing Hands	💧
Washing Clothes	💧💧💧💧💧💧💧

Key 💧 = 10 gallons of water

On Your Own

A class started a recycling project in January. The pictograph below shows how many cans they collected each month. Use your graph-reading skills to find out how well the class did. Remember:

- Read the graph title and labels.

- Study the graph carefully.

- Compare and contrast the information it shows. For example, ask yourself, "In which month did the class collect the most cans?

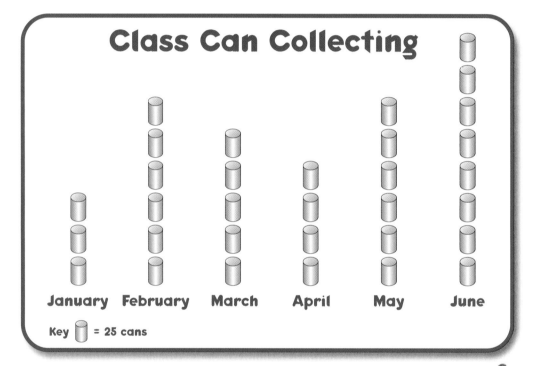

Class Can Collecting

January   February   March   April   May   June

Key ▯ = 25 cans

Write three questions that could be answered by the graph. Use the words and phrases in the list. When you're done, change papers with a partner. Answer each other's questions.

When
In which month
How many
more
less

1. _____

_____

2. _____

_____

3. _____

_____

Text Feature

Graphs

Have you ever heard the expression "A picture is worth a thousand words"? That is really true about a graph! A **graph** is a kind of picture. It shows you **amounts**, or numbers, of things at a glance.

The graph on this page is a **bar graph**. The bars on the graph show an amount, or a number.

Step 1 **Read the title to see what information the graph shows.** The graph below shows how fast five different animals run.

Step 2 **Read the labels on the graph.** The labels on the bottom are *words*. They tell *what* animals the graph is about. The labels on the side are *numbers*. They show *how many* miles per hour.

Step 3 **Find the information that each bar gives.** Move your finger up the bar to where it ends. Then read the number at the side.

Step 4 **Compare and contrast the information on the graph.** Figure out which animal is the fastest, the slowest, which can run twice as fast as another, and so on.

Practice Your Skills!

1. Color in the bar that shows which animal runs the fastest.

2. Circle the two animals that run at about the same speed.

3. How fast does the elephant run?

PAIR SHARE Compare the speeds. Are you surprised by any of them?

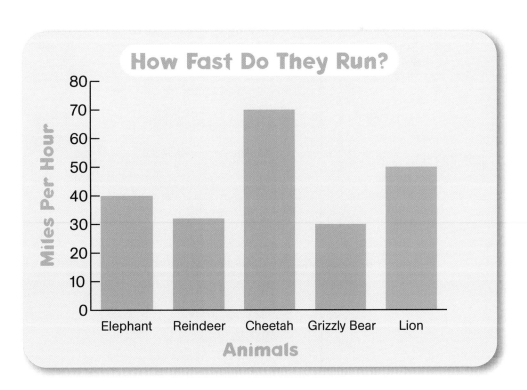

How Fast Do They Run?

Before You Read

Preview the article. Check (✔) the special features it has.

_____ boldfaced words
_____ map
_____ caption
_____ graph
_____ time line

As You Read

- Did you read the title and labels of the graph?
  ❏ Yes ❏ No

- What does the graph show?
  ❏ speed ❏ size

- Where on the graph did you find the speeds?
  ❏ side ❏ bottom

- Explain how you read the bar graph.

After You Read

1. What would make a tennis ball slow down?

2. Which moves faster—a tennis ball or a soccer ball? Why?

PAIR SHARE How does the speed of Venus's serve compare with other tennis serves?

Newsflash

DANGER: High Speed!

Strong players using high-tech rackets are smacking tennis serves faster than ever. The world-record tennis serve is now 149 mph; it's held by Greg Rusedski. Balls that fast are hard to hit back, say experts, making the game boring to watch. Some tennis officials want to slow the game.

How? They could change the size of the ball. As the ball flies, it passes through billions of air particles or **molecules**. The ball rubs against those molecules, causing **friction**, a force that slows the ball. A bigger ball would have more surface area and more friction, so it would travel more slowly. Tennis officials are experimenting with a ball that is just over 2 inches larger in diameter.

Graph questions: Which objects travel at almost the same speed? How much faster than a soccer shot is a hockey shot?

Venus Williams serves up to 125 mph.

Fast Ball

Badminton smash

Tennis serve

Table tennis smash

Ice hockey slapshot

Baseball pitch

Football pass

Soccer shot

| 31 mph | 62 mph | 93 mph | 124 mph | 155 mph | 186 mph | 217 mph |

On Your Own

Make a bar graph to show the average life spans of five different mammals. You can use The Facts at right to help you. Here's how:

- Read the graph title and labels.

- Write the names of the mammals on the lines at the bottom of the graph.

- Use The Facts to make the bars in your graph.

The Facts

The average life span of human beings is 70 years.
The average life span of the Asian elephant is 65 years.
The average life span of the killer whale is 60 years. The average life span of the hippopotamus is 45 years.
The average life span of the rhinoceros is 35 years.

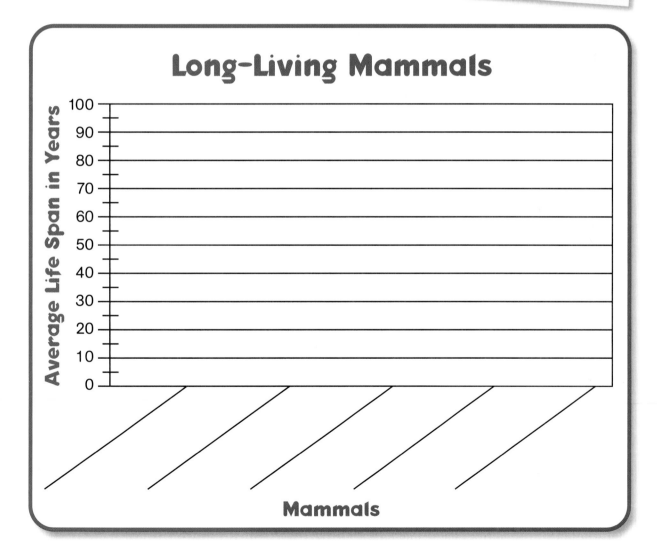

Long-Living Mammals

Average Life Span in Years

100
90
80
70
60
50
40
30
20
10
0

Mammals

The average life span of a human is twice as long as the life span of which mammal?

Compare/Contrast

Practice Your Skills!

Before You Read

Vocabulary Here are some important words from the article. Use the words to fill in the chart.

laws   senators
elect   representatives
Congress

KNOWLEDGE CHART

What We Do	Who They Are	What They Do

As You Read

Text Structure The author of this article **compares and contrasts** the Senate and the House of Representatives. As you read, look for signal words, such as *also* and *however*. Think about how the two groups are alike and how they are different.

Text Feature How does the pictograph help you understand the article?

After You Read

1. Which state has more representatives, New Hampshire or Texas? Why?

2. Which state on the pictograph has the most senators?

3. How are the Senate and the House of Representatives alike? How are they different?

★★★★★★★★★★★★★★★★★★★★★★★★★★

What Is Congress?

★★★★★★★★★★★★★★★★★★★★★★★★★★

★ What Does Congress Do?

Congress makes laws for our country. This is one of its important jobs. Some of our laws are about crime and safety. Other laws are about taxes and money.

Members of Congress meet with people from their states to find out what the people want.

★ Who Is In Congress?

Congress is made up of two groups of people. The two groups are the **Senate** and the **House of Representatives**. Both groups are elected. Each of the 50 states elects two senators who serve in the Senate. There is a total of 100 senators. The people of every state also elect members of the House of Representatives. However, the number of representatives for each state depends on how many people live there. So the total number of representatives is not always the same. It can vary.

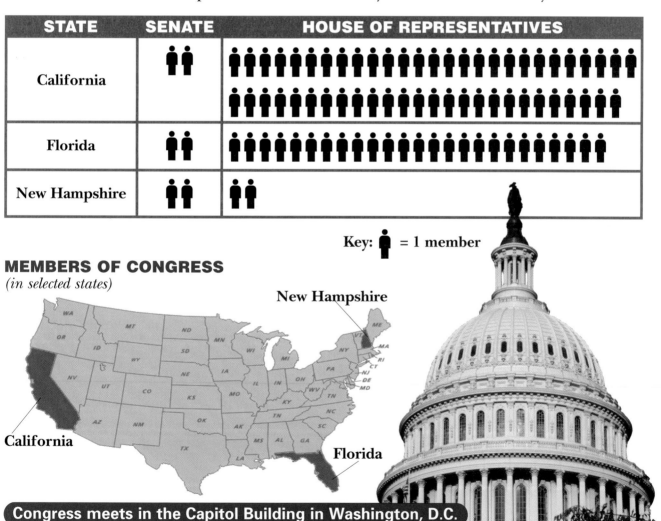

STATE	SENATE	HOUSE OF REPRESENTATIVES
California	🧍🧍	(53 members)
Florida	🧍🧍	(27 members)
New Hampshire	🧍🧍	🧍🧍

Key: 🧍 = 1 member

MEMBERS OF CONGRESS
(in selected states)

New Hampshire

California

Florida

Congress meets in the Capitol Building in Washington, D.C.

Compare/Contrast

Reread "What Is Congress?" Fill in the Venn diagram to compare and contrast the Senate and the House of Representatives. Tell how they are the same and how they are different.

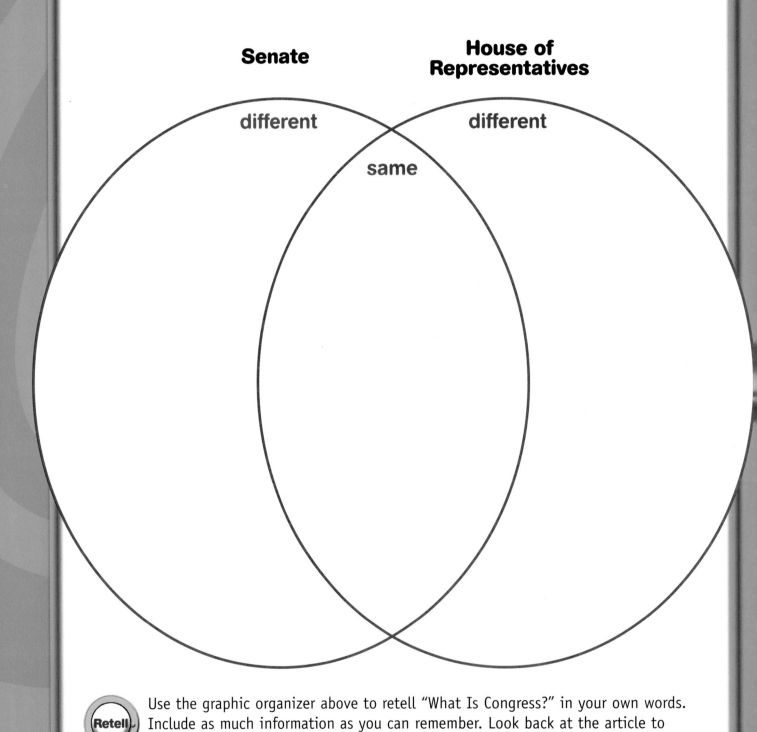

Senate

House of Representatives

different

different

same

Use the graphic organizer above to retell "What Is Congress?" in your own words. Include as much information as you can remember. Look back at the article to help you with details you may have missed.

Retell

Writing Frame

Use the information in your graphic organizer to fill in the writing frame.

Both the _____ and the _____

are the same in some ways. They are the same because they both _____

_____.

They are also the same because they both _____.

Both also _____

_____.

In some ways, though, the _____ and the

_____ are different. They are

different because _____

_____

_____.

So, the _____ and the _____

have both similarities and differences.

 Use the writing frame above as a model to compare and contrast the jobs of mayor and governor. Look in your social studies textbook if you need facts that will help you fill in the frame.

Text Feature

Time Lines

What happened? and *When?* are two questions you might ask when you are learning about a new topic or a famous person. To answer those questions, you could look at a time line. A **time line** is a kind of diagram. It shows real events and the years in which they happened. The information in a time line is always shown in time order. Here's how to read a time line.

Step 1 **Read the title to find out what the time line shows.** The time line below shows the years in which important events first happened in the White House.

Step 2 **Find the starting and ending dates. They tell you how much time is covered.** This time line starts with the year 1800 and goes to the year 2000. How many years is that?

Step 3 **Look at the dates in between. They appear in time order and tell you the year when each event took place.** Only the years when something important took place are shown.

Step 4 **Read the caption for each date. It tells what happened.** A line connects the date to a picture and a caption about the event.

Practice Your Skills!

1. Circle the year in which the White House first got running water.

2. Until 1891, the White House did not have _____.

3. What is one event that took place during your lifetime?

PAIR SHARE How old is the White House? How can you tell?

White House Firsts

1833 White House first gets running water.

1947 The first TV speech is made from the White House.

2000 The first time a millennium is celebrated in the White House.

1891 White House first gets electric lights.

1800 1820 1840 1860 1880 1900 1920 1940 1960 1980 2000

1879 White House gets its first telephone.

1800 The building of the White House is finished. John Adams is the first President to live there.

1909 White House gets its first cars.

1965 White House gets its first fire alarm.

Before You Read

Preview the article. Check (✔) the special features it has.

_____ title
_____ headings
_____ captions
_____ introduction
_____ time line

As You Read

• Did you read the title of the time line?
❏ Yes ❏ No

• Did you figure out how much time was covered?
❏ Yes ❏ No

• Did you read the dates and captions in order?
❏ Yes ❏ No

• Explain how you read the time line.

After You Read

1. What were three important things Washington did in his lifetime?

2. How does the time line help you understand and remember what was in the article?

PAIR SHARE Why do you think Washington read the Declaration of Independence to his troops?

TO LEAD A NEW NATION

Washington is being sworn in as president. He took an oath, promising to protect and defend the laws of the U.S.

Hail to the chief! On April 30, 1789, George Washington became the first President of the United States. He took his oath of office in New York City, the nation's capital at that time.

Wartime Leader

Our nation was once a group of **colonies**, territories owned by another country— England. In 1776, the colonies decided to become a separate nation. England tried to stop that from happening. A war broke out. It was called the Revolutionary War.

During the war, Washington was commander in chief of the Continental Army. He and his troops defeated the British in 1781. The U.S. became a free and independent nation.

Peacetime Leader

In 1787, Washington was asked to lead a very important meeting in Pennsylvania. At this meeting, called the Constitutional Convention, leaders from the 13 colonies gathered to write a set of laws for the new nation. These laws are the United States Constitution.

Everyone at the meeting agreed that Washington should be the first president of the new country. In that role, it was up to him to set an example for all future presidents of how best to do the job.

1732	Born in the colony of Virginia.
1758	Elected to be a representative in the government of the colony of Virginia.
1775	The Revolutionary War began. Washington is named commander in chief of the colony's army.
1776	The Declaration of Independence was written. Washington read it to his troops.
1781	Washington and his troops won an important battle.
1783	England and the U.S. signed a peace treaty. Washington left the army and went back to Mount Vernon.
1787	Went to the Continental Congress as a delegate from Virginia.
1788	All electors from every state chose Washington to be the first president.
1792	Washington was elected to a second term as president. Four years later, he refused a third term.
1799	Died at Mount Vernon.

On Your Own

Benjamin Franklin was another important person in the history of our country. The Facts tells you something about his life. Read it and then make a time line. Choose what you think are the most important events.

1. In the text, circle the first and last dates you want to include.

2. Write the dates at the beginning and end of the time line with a caption about what happened on each date.

3. Go back to the text and circle the other events you want to include. Add the information to the time line.

4. Think about what you already know: What other great American lived at the same time as Benjamin Franklin?

The Facts

Benjamin Franklin was born in 1706 in Boston, Massachusetts. He was the 15th of 17 children. When he was a young man, he learned to be a printer by working with his brother James. In 1723, he set up his own print shop in Philadelphia. There, in 1733, he published his famous book of wise sayings, *Poor Richard's Almanac.*

Franklin was an inventor as well as a printer. He invented the Franklin stove in 1744 and bifocal glasses ten years later. And in 1752, using a kite, he showed that lightning is electricity.

But Ben Franklin may best be remembered for the part he played in making our country independent from England. Franklin helped write the Declaration of Independence in 1776. He attended the Constitutional Convention in 1787, where he was one of the writers of the U.S. Constitution. Benjamin Franklin died in 1790.

Benjamin Franklin

Text Feature

Time Lines

A **time line** is a diagram that shows a series of real events and the dates when they happened. The information in a time line is always shown in time order, from the earliest date to the latest.

Step 1 **Read the title to find out what the time line shows.**
The time line below shows when certain sports and games were first played.

Step 2 **Find the starting and ending dates. They tell you how much time is covered.** This time line begins with the year 1611 and ends with 2000. That's 389 years.

Step 3 **Look at all the dates. They appear in time order and tell you the year when each event took place.**
Not every year of the 389 years is shown. Only the years when certain sports were introduced appear.

Step 4 **Read the label for each date. It tells what happened.**
A line connects each year to the event that took place.

Practice Your Skills!

1. Circle the dates that show when two kinds of sports equipment were invented.

2. Underline the events that tell about the invention of new sports.

PAIR SHARE What sports have been played in our country for 200 years or more? Are you surprised that any of them are so old? Why or why not?

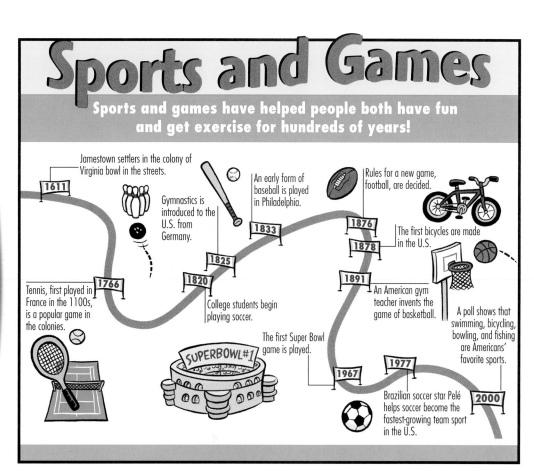

Sports and Games

Sports and games have helped people both have fun and get exercise for hundreds of years!

1611 Jamestown settlers in the colony of Virginia bowl in the streets.

Gymnastics is introduced to the U.S. from Germany.

1833 An early form of baseball is played in Philadelphia.

1876 Rules for a new game, football, are decided.

1878 The first bicycles are made in the U.S.

1766 Tennis, first played in France in the 1100s, is a popular game in the colonies.

1825 **1820** College students begin playing soccer.

1891 An American gym teacher invents the game of basketball.

A poll shows that swimming, bicycling, bowling, and fishing are Americans' favorite sports.

The first Super Bowl game is played.

SUPERBOWL #1

1967 **1977** **2000**

Brazilian soccer star Pelé helps soccer become the fastest-growing team sport in the U.S.

Before You Read

Preview the article. Check (✔) the special features it has.

____ time line
____ map
____ labels
____ boldfaced words
____ chart

As You Read

• Did you find out what the time line is about?
❏ Yes ❏ No

• How many years are covered on the time line?

• Did you understand how certain inventions led to others?

• Explain how you read the time line.

After You Read

1. What happens when an electric current is not moving?

2. What invention made skyscrapers possible?

3. Which inventions were made during your lifetime?

PAIR SHARE How is this time line different from the one about George Washington?

It's Electric!

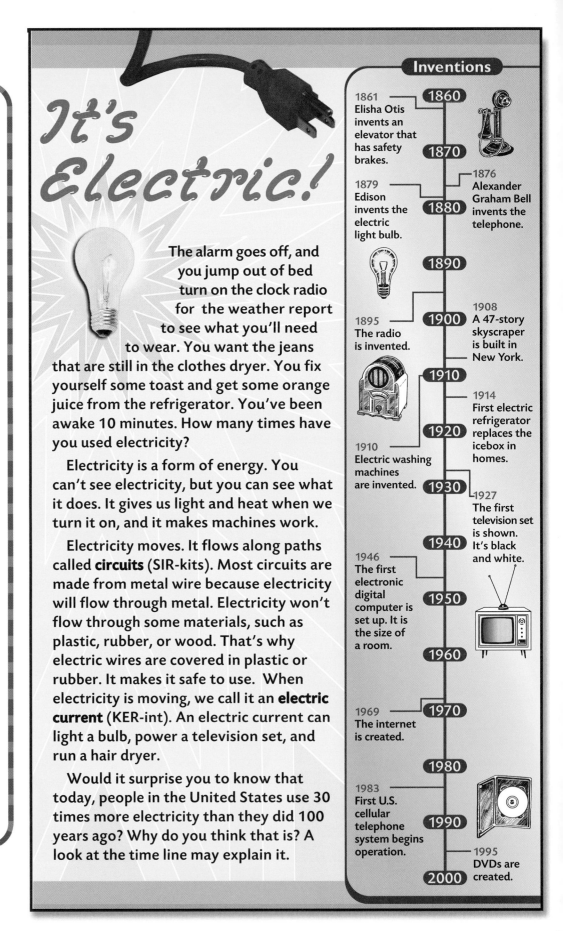

The alarm goes off, and you jump out of bed turn on the clock radio for the weather report to see what you'll need to wear. You want the jeans that are still in the clothes dryer. You fix yourself some toast and get some orange juice from the refrigerator. You've been awake 10 minutes. How many times have you used electricity?

Electricity is a form of energy. You can't see electricity, but you can see what it does. It gives us light and heat when we turn it on, and it makes machines work.

Electricity moves. It flows along paths called **circuits** (SIR-kits). Most circuits are made from metal wire because electricity will flow through metal. Electricity won't flow through some materials, such as plastic, rubber, or wood. That's why electric wires are covered in plastic or rubber. It makes it safe to use. When electricity is moving, we call it an **electric current** (KER-int). An electric current can light a bulb, power a television set, and run a hair dryer.

Would it surprise you to know that today, people in the United States use 30 times more electricity than they did 100 years ago? Why do you think that is? A look at the time line may explain it.

Inventions

1861 Elisha Otis invents an elevator that has safety brakes.

1860

1870

1876 Alexander Graham Bell invents the telephone.

1879 Edison invents the electric light bulb.

1880

1890

1895 The radio is invented.

1900

1908 A 47-story skyscraper is built in New York.

1910

1914 First electric refrigerator replaces the icebox in homes.

1910 Electric washing machines are invented.

1920

1930

1927 The first television set is shown. It's black and white.

1940

1946 The first electronic digital computer is set up. It is the size of a room.

1950

1960

1969 The internet is created.

1970

1980

1983 First U.S. cellular telephone system begins operation.

1990

1995 DVDs are created.

2000

On Your Own

Make a time line about someone you know very well—yourself! Your time line could start with the day you were born and continue through this year. Or you could focus on what happened during the months of just one year.

- Figure out the length of time you are going to cover. Put the earliest date at the beginning of your time line and the latest date at the other end.

- Write the dates, in time order, that you are going to include on the time line. Draw a line from the date to the time line. Then write a caption to tell what happened on each date.

- Add drawings or photos, if you would like to.

 Write three questions that can be answered by your time line. Use the words and phrases in the list. When you're finished, change papers with a partner. Answer each other's questions.

When
In which year
In which month
What happened on
How many years before
How many years after

1._____

_____

2._____

_____

3._____

_____

Problem/Solution

Before You Read

Vocabulary Write the words and phrases where they belong in the chart.

civil rights   equality
segregation   prejudice

Dr. King was against	Dr. King worked for

As You Read

Text Structure The article tells about the problems African Americans had. It also tells what Dr. Martin Luther King, Jr., did to help solve those problems. To keep track of the information, underline in red the key words that tell about the problem. Underline in black the solutions.

Text Feature How does the time line help you understand the article?

After You Read

1. How is Martin Luther King III like his father?

2. Study the time line. How many years ago did it become illegal to keep whites and African Americans separated in public schools?

3. What did you already know about Dr. Martin Luther King, Jr.? What new things did you learn from the article?

Martin Luther King III toda[y]

Dr. King pitches to his son, Martin Luther King III.

A Boy and His Father

As a young boy, Martin Luther King III liked to play sports with his father, Dr. Martin Luther King, Jr. They swam and rode bikes together. "We also played baseball in the backyard," Martin says. However, the Kings were not free to do all the things they enjoyed where they lived in Atlanta, Georgia.

At that time, laws in the south **segregated**, or separated, whites and African Americans. African Americans had to sit in separate sections in movie theaters and on buses and go to separate restaurants and swimming pools. These same laws also kept children of different races from attending the same schools.

Dr. King worked to change unfair laws like these. He led peaceful marches of protest and gave many speeches. "He traveled a lot to fight **prejudice** in different places in the country," Martin Luther King III says.

His Father's Dream

Because of Dr. King's work, many people joined in the protests. In 1963, thousands of people, marching for **civil rights**, gathered in Washington, D.C. They heard Dr. King give his most famous speech. He said, "I have a dream that my four little children will one day not be judged by the color of their skin, but by the content of their character." Dr. King convinced, or proved to, most Americans that all people should be treated equally and fairly. As a result, the laws began to change. When Martin Luther King III was in the third grade, he was one of the first African-American children in the South to go to school with white children. Dr. King saw that his dream was beginning to come true. However, there was still a lot to be done.

The Son Today

In 1968, Dr. King was in Tennessee continuing his fight for **equality**. There, he was assassinated, or killed. Today, his son, Martin Luther King III, leads a group that was started by his father. The group works for peace and equality. They want to make America a better place for all people.

"Have hope!" Martin says. "By working together as one community, we can solve our problems."

Dr. Martin Luther King, Jr.

More than 200,000 people heard Martin Luther King, Jr., give his famous "I Have a Dream" speech.

MAJOR EVENTS IN CIVIL RIGHTS

1725	About 75,000 enslaved Africans live in the English colonies.
1775	The first group that wanted to end slavery is formed in Philadelphia.
1849	Harriet Tubman escapes from slavery. She will take more than 300 slaves to freedom on the Underground Railroad.
1863	All slaves in the U.S. are given their freedom by President Abraham Lincoln.
1870	Two African Americans are elected to Congress for the first time.
1915	Thousands of African Americans move from the South to the North looking for jobs and better education.
1947	Jackie Robinson becomes the first African-American baseball player in the Major Leagues.
1954	Supreme Court of the U.S. says that having separate public schools for blacks and whites is against the law.
1955	Dr. Martin Luther King, Jr., and others lead protests against segregation in the South. The protests continue for many years.
1963	Dr. Martin Luther King, Jr., makes his "I Have a Dream" speech in Washington, D.C.
1964	Congress passes a law that makes it illegal to prevent people from voting or getting a job because of their race or religion.
1968	Dr. Martin Luther King, Jr., is shot and killed.
1983	The third Monday in January becomes a holiday to honor Dr. King.
1992	Mae Jemison is the first African-American woman in space.
2001	Colin Powell becomes the first African American to serve as U.S. Secretary of State.

Problem/Solution

Reread "A Son Remembers." Fill in the graphic organizer. First, identify the problems that were discussed in the article. Then, fill in the steps Dr. King took to solve the problems. Finally, use both the article and the information in the time line to tell what finally happened to help solve the problems.

Problems

Dr. King's Solutions

What Finally Happened

 Use the graphic organizer above to retell "A Son Remembers" in your own words. Include as much information as you can remember. Look back at the article to help you with any details that you may have missed.

Writing Frame

Use the information in your graphic organizer to fill in the writing frame.

When Martin Luther King III was a boy, the problem was that his family

was not free to do the things white people could do. This happened because

_____

_____.

For example,_____

_____

_____

_____.

Many things helped to solve the problem. Some of them were that

_____

_____

_____

_____.

Today, Martin Luther King III works for peace and equality, just like his

father did.

 Use the writing frame above as a model to write about a problem in the environment and what people are doing to solve the problem. Look in your social studies textbook if you need facts that will help you fill in the frame.

Text Feature

Charts

You'll see charts in textbooks, magazines, and on the sports pages of newspapers. A **chart** is a special graphic aid, set up like a table, that shows facts about a topic. For example, a chart can show the population of large U.S. cities or name each state's bird. The chart organizes the information and makes it easy to understand. It can show a lot of information without using a lot of words.

Step 1 **Read the title and introduction to find out what the chart shows.** The chart below shows several U.S. state names that come from Native American words.

Step 2 **Read the headings on the columns.** The column headings tell us what type of information we will find in each column.

Step 3 **Read the information in each column, from left to right.** For example, the name **Utah** comes from a Navajo word meaning "high up."

Practice Your Skills!

1. Put an **X** on the title of the chart.

2. Circle the heading in each column.

3. Which state name comes from an Iroquois word?

PAIR SHARE Why do you think each state name was chosen? How does the name tell something about the state?

Native American State Names

Did you know that 28 states in the U.S. got their names from Native American words? Here are just a few.

STATE	LANGUAGE	WHAT IT MEANS
Alaska	Aleutian	"land that is not an island"
Connecticut	Mahican	"long river place"
Kansas	Sioux	"south-wind people"
Missouri	Algonquin	"river of the big canoes"
Ohio	Iroquois	"good river"
Utah	Navajo	"high up"
Wyoming	Algonquin	"large prairie place"

Practice Your Skills!

Before You Read

Preview the article. Check (✔) the special features it has.

_____ pronunciations
_____ boldfaced words
_____ chart
_____ map key
_____ headings

As You Read

- Did you read the title of the chart?
  ❏ Yes ❏ No

- Did you read the chart's caption?
  ❏ Yes ❏ No

- Did you read the boldfaced words in the article and think about their meanings?
  ❏ Yes ❏ No

- Explain how you read the chart.

After You Read

1. Which animal will represent 2014?

2. What are three examples of Chinese culture?

PAIR SHARE How is the Chinese calendar different from the calendar you use?

≋ CHINESE NEW YEAR ≋

May You Prosper!

Gung hay fat choy! May you prosper! This is the Chinese greeting for the New Year. In China, New Year is the most important holiday. It is celebrated by Chinese people all over the world.

The date of Chinese New Year is not January 1. In fact, the New Year begins on a different day each year. It is sometime between January 21 and February 19. Why is that? The Chinese calendar is based on the **phases** of the moon. These phases are changes in the moon's shape as it looks to us from Earth.

Chinese New Year begins when the moon is in the "new moon" phase. During this phase, the moon cannot be seen. The celebrations end 15 days later, when the full moon lights the sky.

Chinese New Year in the U.S.

LOS ANGELES, CALIFORNIA

Los Angeles has had a Chinese New Year Parade every year for 104 years!

A huge painted dragon, swaying back and forth, starts off the parade. The dragon is the symbol of power, luck, strength, and success. It is followed by floats, marching bands, and drummers. People from all over the country come to the colorful parade. It's easy to see why!

PORTLAND, MAINE

Portland celebrates Chinese New Year with a fair. Children show their talents, such as spinning handkerchiefs on their fingers. It's traditional. Some children learned how in China.

People at the fair learn about Chinese **culture**, or the Chinese way of life. They will hear Chinese music, play Chinese games, and eat Chinese food.

Chinese Calendar

Each year on the Chinese calendar is named for 1 of 12 animals. The chart shows the animals and the years they represent.

Boar — Honorable and brave. 1995 2007
Rat — Honest and ambitious. 1996 2008
Ox — Bright and patient. 1997 2009
Tiger — Courageous and sensitive. 1998 2010
Rabbit — Luckiest of all. Talented and loving. 1999 2011
Dragon — Proud and energetic. 2000 2012
Snake — Wise and good looking. 2001 2013
Horse — Popular and attractive. 2002
Ram — Elegant and creative. 1991 2003
Monkey — Smart and funny. 1992 2004
Rooster — Honest and adventurous. 1993 2005
Dog — Loyal and honest. 1994 2006

On Your Own

Read the paragraphs below. Then use the information to fill in the chart.

Holidays

Many holidays are celebrated during the same time of year. Ramadan is a monthlong holiday. It is a special religious time for the Islamic people. It is celebrated sometime between mid-October and mid-November. Adults observe the holiday by fasting, or not eating, during the daylight hours.

Hanukkah is the Jewish festival of lights. It lasts for eight days. It is celebrated sometime in December. Families celebrate by lighting candles on a menorah, or special candleholder, each night.

Las Posadas is a Mexican holiday that is celebrated in the days leading up to Christmas. The Mexican people end the nine-day celebration by breaking a piñata filled with special treats.

Holiday Season

Holiday	Las Posadas	Ramadan	Hanukkah
Who Celebrates			
Key Facts			

Text Feature

Charts

Many science books contain charts to go with the text. A **chart** is a special graphic aid that shows facts about a topic. The chart organizes the information. A chart also makes it easy for you to compare and contrast the facts at a glance.

Step 1 **Read the title to find out what the chart shows.**
The chart below shows facts about each planet and its moons.

Step 2 **Read the headings on the columns.** The column headings tell us the type of information we will find in each column.

Step 3 **Read the information in each column, from left to right.**
For example, Mars has only two moons.
They are named Deimos and Phobos.

No Two Planets Are Alike

Planet	Number of Known Moons*	Interesting Facts About the Moons
Mercury	0	Mercury has no moons.
Venus	0	Venus has no moons.
Earth	1	The spacecraft *Lunar Prospector* discovered that Earth's moon has lots of ice at its poles and a small core at its center.
Mars	2	One moon, Deimos, is one of the smallest in the solar system; the other, Phobos, will someday crash into Mars.
Jupiter	16	Jupiter's moon Ganymede, the largest moon in the solar system, is surrounded by dust caused by meteorites hitting its surface.
Saturn	18	Saturn's moon Titan, the second largest in the solar system, has a thick atmosphere filled with orange clouds.
Uranus	18	The spacecraft *Voyager 2* discovered 10 moons when it visited Uranus in 1986.
Neptune	8	Neptune's moon Triton orbits its planet in a clockwise direction, unlike other big moons in the solar system.

*(as of 2003)

Practice Your Skills!

1. Circle the title of the chart.

2. Put an **X** on each heading to learn the main ideas.

3. Underline the name of each planet that has more than two moons.

PAIR SHARE What is different about each planet's moons?

Before You Read

Preview the article. Check (✔) the special features it has.

_____ boldfaced words
_____ pronunciations
_____ chart
_____ headings
_____ diagram

As You Read

• Did you read the title of the chart?
  ❏ Yes ❏ No

• Did you read the chart's headings?
  ❏ Yes ❏ No

• Did you read the boldfaced words in the article and think about their meanings?
  ❏ Yes ❏ No

• Explain how you read the chart.

After You Read

1. Which space object is a lot like Pluto? Why?

2. What word means "facts that help prove something"?

 Do you think Pluto should be called a planet? Why or why not?

PLUTO ROCKS!

This picture shows what the surface of Pluto is believed to look like. You can see Pluto's moon on the left and the sun on the right.

Since its discovery in 1930, Pluto has been called the ninth planet of our solar system. Now, some experts say the farthest planet from the sun is not a planet at all.

Here's why: A planet is usually described as a large, round body that circles the sun. Some scientists think Pluto is too small to be a planet. They believe it's just an icy rock in an area near our solar system called the Kuiper (KY-per) Belt. This **region**, or area, is loaded with objects made of rock and ice that are too small to be planets.

Scientists who believe that Pluto isn't a planet recently found **evidence**, or facts that help prove

something. Using a telescope, scientists discovered an object called Quaoar (KWAH-o-ar) in the Kuiper Belt. Quaoar is a lot like Pluto. They are both made of ice and rock, and both circle the sun. Scientists think they are so similar they must be the same kind of space object. They say if Quaoar is not a planet, Pluto shouldn't be called one either.

"Quaoar definitely hurts the case for Pluto being a planet," says Mike Brown, who helped discover Quaoar.

So is Pluto a planet? In 2006, the International Astronomical Union decided on a new category for Pluto. They call it a "dwarf planet."

Pluto and Earth: Worlds Apart

	Earth	**Pluto**
AVERAGE TEMPERATURE	The average temperature of the Earth's surface is 59 degrees Fahrenheit.	The average temperature of Pluto's surface is –369 degrees Fahrenheit. (Brrr!)
LENGTH OF DAYS	One day is 24 hours.	One day is 153 hours.
WEIGHT	If you weigh 60 pounds on Earth…	…you would weigh 3 ½ pounds on Pluto.

On Your Own

Read about Mars and Jupiter below. Use the information to complete the chart.

Mars

Mars is the fourth planet from the sun. It is nicknamed the "Red Planet" because of its rust color. It was named after the Roman god of war. The average temperature on Mars is –81 degrees Fahrenheit. One day on Mars is almost the same as one day on Earth. If you weighed 60 pounds on Earth, you would weigh 23 pounds on Mars.

Jupiter

Jupiter is the fifth planet from the sun. It is the largest planet in our solar system. It was named after the leader of the Roman gods. The average temperature on Jupiter is –224 degrees Fahrenheit. One day on Jupiter lasts about 10 hours. If you weighed 60 pounds on Earth, you would weigh 152 pounds on Jupiter.

•••••••••••••••••••••••••• **Planets Near and Far** ••••••••••••••••••••••••••

The chart below shows some important—and fun— differences between Earth, Mars, and Jupiter.

	Earth	Mars	Jupiter
AVERAGE TEMPERATURE	The average temperature of the Earth's surface is 59 degrees Fahrenheit.		
LENGTH OF DAYS	One day is 24 hours.		
WEIGHT	If you weigh 60 pounds on Earth...		
INTERESTING FACT	We live here.		

Cause/Effect

Before You Read

Vocabulary Here are some important words from the article. Read the definitions. Then use the sentence starters to discuss each word.

recycle: to use again
Every week we recycle _____ .

conserve: to save
To conserve water and energy, we can _____ .

As You Read

Text Structure This article discusses why the earth's animals need our help in cleaning up and saving resources. What we do can **cause** good **effects**. The effects of protecting the earth's natural resources are in the column labeled *How It Helps*.

Text Feature How does the format of the article help you read it? Why did the author make the article a chart?

After You Read

1. What will happen if you use less paper?

2. Why is turning off the water while you brush your teeth a good thing to do?

3. Which of these do you do in your community? What else might you do?

Helping
You can do things

What You Can Do *(cause)*

You can clean up your trash at the beach. Clean up any other trash you find, too.

You can use less paper. You can also recycle paper.

You can conserve water by turning off the faucet when you brush your teeth.

How It Helps (effect)

Trash can get into the ocean. When pelicans dive for fish, they can pick up trash instead. As a result, the trash gets caught around the pelicans' necks and hurts them. That doesn't happen when people clean up the trash.

Paper is made from trees. Therefore, when you use less paper, people cut down fewer trees. That leaves plenty of trees for animals like squirrels to live in.

Conserving water leaves more clean water in rivers. Animals like otters live in the rivers. Therefore, it's important to keep this otter's home full of clean water.

Cause/Effect

Reread "Helping Earth's Animals." Fill in the chart to show either the cause or the effect.

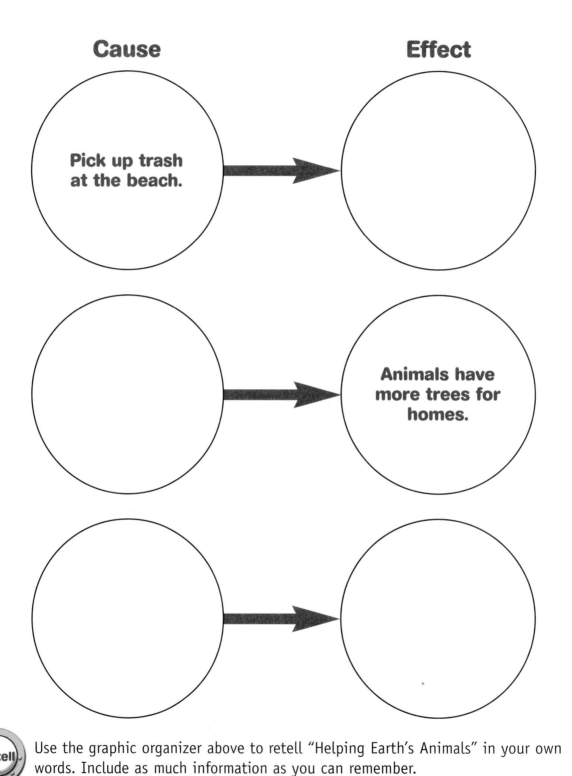

Cause

Effect

Pick up trash at the beach.

Animals have more trees for homes.

Use the graphic organizer above to retell "Helping Earth's Animals" in your own words. Include as much information as you can remember.

Retell

Writing Frame

Use the information in your graphic organizer to fill in the writing frame.

Many of Earth's animals are in danger. There are several things we can do

to help them.

We can _____.

The effect of this is _____

_____.

We can also _____.

The effect of this is _____

_____.

In addition, we can _____

_____. The effect of this is _____

_____.

Therefore, it's important to help Earth's animals so that they _____

_____.

Use the writing frame above as a model to write a paragraph about helping your community. Begin like this, "We can do a lot to help our community." Look in your science textbook or local newspaper if you need facts that will help you.

Text Feature

Maps

A **map** is a flat picture of part of Earth. Social studies textbooks contain many types of maps. A **physical map** shows Earth's natural features, such as mountains, oceans, and rivers. A **political map** shows facts about countries, states, and cities. These maps help you picture the place that is being described.

Step 1 **Read the map title. It tells you what the map is about.** The map below shows the regions of the U.S. and the biggest cities in each. It's a political map.

Step 2 **Find the map symbols.** A symbol stands for a real thing or place. It may be a picture or a special color.

Step 3 **Look at the map key or legend. It tells you what each map symbol means.** In the map below, a dot stands for a city.

Step 4 **Read the map labels.** They tell the names of cities, states, regions, countries, oceans, and other places.

Step 5 **Find the compass rose.** It shows the directions on the map. **N** stands for north, **S** stands for south, **E** stands for east, and **W** stands for west.

Practice Your Skills!

1. How many regions are shown on the map?

2. Put an **X** on the biggest city in the West region.

3. Circle the name of the region in which Dallas can be found.

PAIR SHARE Which states have the biggest cities? Which of these cities have you visited or seen on TV?

REGIONS OF THE U.S.

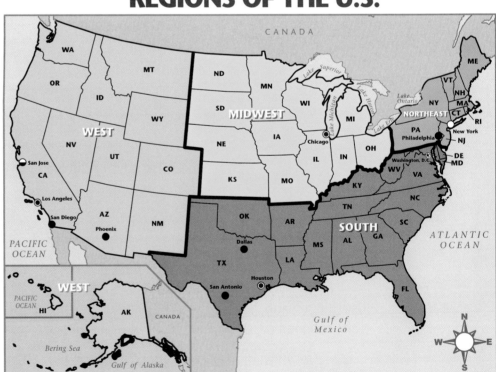

KEY

— Regional division

— State border

Population of the 10 Largest U.S. Cities

○ More than 4 million

◉ 2 to 4 million

● 1 to 2 million

◒ less than 1 million

Source: U.S. Census Bureau. Data based on July 1, 2004 population estimates.

Before You Read

Preview the article. Check (✔) the special features it has.

_____ caption
_____ headings
_____ graph
_____ boldfaced words
_____ map

As You Read

• Did you read the title of the map? ❏ Yes ❏ No

• Did you read all the map labels? ❏ Yes ❏ No

• Did you compare the numbers in each label? ❏ Yes ❏ No

• Explain what you learned from reading the map.

After You Read

1. Which state has the most Native American tribes?

2. What does *culture* mean? What are some examples of your culture?

PAIR SHARE What is the weather like in the regions with the most tribes? How might that affect the way the tribes live?

Powwow Now

Sequoya (suh-KWOI-uh) Reels likes action. He likes football, karate, and playing with his brothers at his home in Connecticut. Every year, Sequoya and his family go to a big Native American **festival**, or celebration, called a *powwow*. There is plenty of action going on there.

Sounds and Colors

At a powwow, Sequoya says, "We get to celebrate our **culture**," or way of life. People sing and dance while drummers play. "It's really loud because of the drums," Sequoya says.

He joins other boys his age in a dance full of quick steps and spins. It is called the "fancy dance" because of the dancers' fast movements and colorful clothes. Sequoya wears white and purple, the colors of his tribe. He is a member of the Mashantucket Pequot (MASH-ahn-TUHK-et PEE-kwot) tribe.

A Special Gathering

Long ago, each different Native American group held its own powwows, as meetings or celebrations. Today, people from many tribes gather at the same powwow to enjoy Native American crafts, food, and music.

Today, the powwow at the Mashantucket Pequot reservation attracts more than 3,000 dancers, drummers, and singers from 500 tribal nations.

U.S. States With the Most Tribes

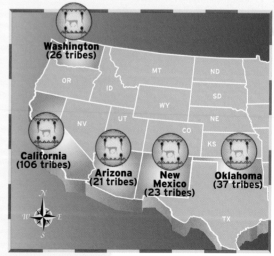

Washington (26 tribes)
California (106 tribes)
Arizona (21 tribes)
New Mexico (23 tribes)
Oklahoma (37 tribes)

On Your Own

Complete the map to show how many American Indians live in each state. Read The Facts. Then use the key to figure out the colors to use.

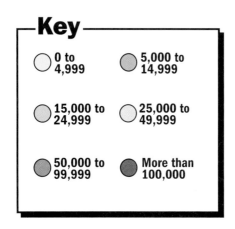

Key

- ⚪ 0 to 4,999
- ⚪ 5,000 to 14,999
- ⚪ 15,000 to 24,999
- ⚪ 25,000 to 49,999
- ⚪ 50,000 to 99,999
- ⚫ More than 100,000

The Facts

1. Texas has more than 100,000 American Indians.
2. Florida has over 50,000 American Indians living there, but less than 100,000.
3. West Virginia has less than 5,000 American Indians.
4. Wisconsin has less than 15,000 American Indians living in the state, but more than West Virginia.

American Indian Population

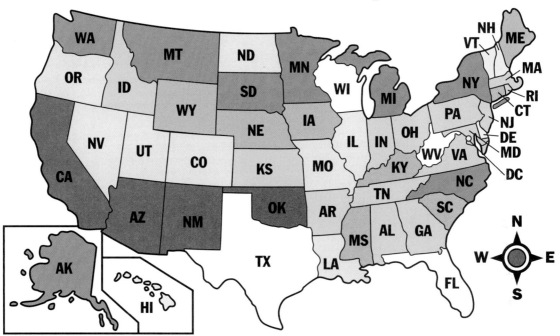

How many American Indians live in your state? _____

Text Feature

Maps

A **map** is a flat picture of part of Earth. Science books contain many types of maps. Below is a weather map of Florida. Here's how to read it:

Step 1 **Read the map title. It tells you what the map is about.** The map below shows one U.S. state.

Step 2 **Find the map symbols.** A symbol stands for a real thing or place. It may be a picture or a special color.

Step 3 **Look at the map key to see what each symbol means.**

Step 4 **Read the labels on the map.** These words tell the names of cities, states, countries, bodies of water, and other places.

Step 5 **Find the compass rose.** It shows the directions on the map. **N** stands for north, **S** stands for south, **E** stands for east, and **W** stands for west.

Practice Your Skills!

1. Put an **X** on the state's capital city.

2. Circle the map key.

3. What's the weather like in the northern part of the state?

PAIR SHARE Why would someone find this map important?

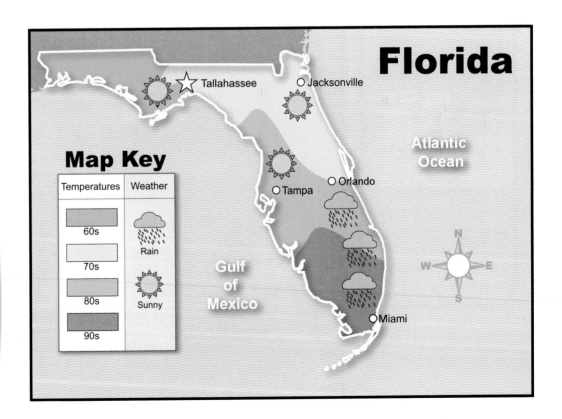

Map Key

Temperatures	Weather
60s	Rain
70s	
80s	Sunny
90s	

Florida

Tallahassee · Jacksonville · Tampa · Orlando · Miami

Atlantic Ocean

Gulf of Mexico

Before You Read

Preview the article. Check (✔) the special features it has.

_____ title
_____ time line
_____ headings
_____ graph
_____ map

As You Read

• Did you read the title of the map?
❑ Yes ❑ No

• Did you read all the map labels?
❑ Yes ❑ No

• Did you trace the path of the hurricane with your finger? ❑ Yes ❑ No

• Explain what you learned from reading the map.

After You Read

1. When does hurricane season begin?

2. What is another word for _region_?

PAIR SHARE What happens when a hurricane comes on to land? Why?

HURRICANE HUNT

When September arrives, it is the height of hurricane season. Experts predict the number of these powerful storms that will occur each year.

Hurricanes happen when the weather is warm. In the Atlantic Ocean **region**, or area, hurricane season begins on June 1 and ends on November 30.

On the Move

Hurricanes begin as a **cluster**, or group, of thunderstorms that move across the ocean. These storms carry heavy rains and strong winds.

When the winds reach more than 74 miles per hour, the storm becomes a hurricane. Hurricane winds can reach 155 miles per hour and can destroy trees, cars, and homes.

The Right Track

Weather experts can find hurricanes before they arrive. They use satellites and airplanes to track a storm and to measure its wind speed. If a hurricane is near land, the experts can warn people to take shelter ahead of time. Each year, their work saves many lives.

LEVEL	WIND SPEED	DAMAGE
1	74–95 miles per hour	Destroys plants and crops
2	96–110 miles per hour	Breaks windows, blows trees down
3	111–130 miles per hour	Damages roofs, floods coastline
4	131–155 miles per hour	Rips roofs and doors off
5	155 miles per hour	Wrecks houses and buildings

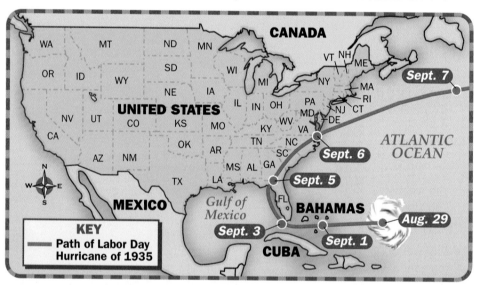

KEY
— Path of Labor Day Hurricane of 1935

Top 5 Hurricane States in the U.S.

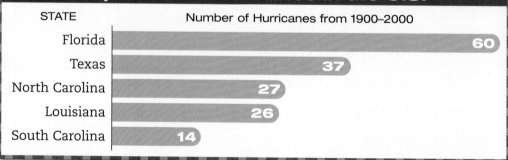

STATE	Number of Hurricanes from 1900–2000
Florida	60
Texas	37
North Carolina	27
Louisiana	26
South Carolina	14

On Your Own

Look at the State Weather Watch map. Study the map key and think about the information the map contains. Then, add the following information:

- It is snowing in Minneapolis, Minnesota.
- It is stormy in Arizona.
- It is raining in Chicago.
- It is sunny on the East Coast.

State Weather Watch
A weather map shows the weather in different places.

 Read the questions below. Put a ✔ in front of each question that can be answered by the map. Then, write another question about the map. When you're done, change papers with a partner. Answer each other's questions.

❑ 1. Where was it raining on March 7?

❑ 2. What is the average temperature of Chicago in March?

❑ 3. Was it hot in Memphis on March 7?

4. My own question _____

_____

Description

Practice Your Skills!

Before You Read

Vocabulary Tell how the word pairs in the chart are related. Use the two words in a sentence.

Related Word Pairs
ancient/traditions
population/citizens

As You Read

Text Structure The author of this article **describes**, or tells about, kids from Spanish-speaking nations. As you read, circle the name of the place each child is from. Find it on the map.

Text Feature How does the map help you understand the article?

After You Read

1. Why do people in all these places speak Spanish?

2. Study the map. Which Spanish-speaking nation is in North America? How does that fact help you better understand the pie chart?

3. What do all these kids have in common? What is different about the place each is from?

One Language,

What's in a name? When you say Latino, or Hispanic, there's more than you might think! Latinos come from many nations, each with its own history, traditions, foods, and way of life. However, these nations do share one thing: the Spanish language. That's because they were all settled by people who came from Spain hundreds of years ago. Read what these kids have to say about where their families came from.

This is a circle graph, or pie chart. It shows the top five states where Latinos live in the United States. The state with the biggest piece of the pie is California. That's because California has the largest Latino population in the country.

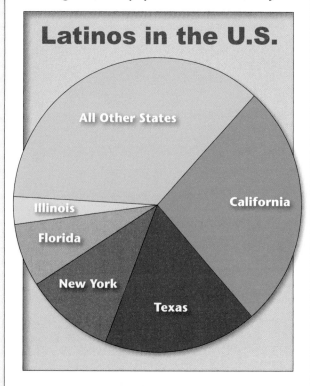

Latinos in the U.S.

All Other States

Illinois

Florida

New York

Texas

California

Many Nations

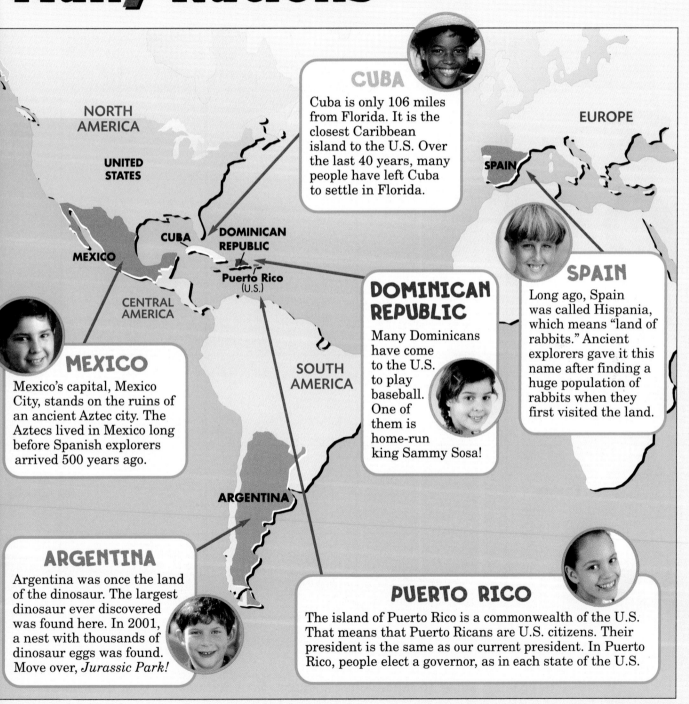

CUBA

Cuba is only 106 miles from Florida. It is the closest Caribbean island to the U.S. Over the last 40 years, many people have left Cuba to settle in Florida.

NORTH AMERICA

UNITED STATES

EUROPE

SPAIN

CUBA

DOMINICAN REPUBLIC

Puerto Rico (U.S.)

MEXICO

CENTRAL AMERICA

MEXICO

Mexico's capital, Mexico City, stands on the ruins of an ancient Aztec city. The Aztecs lived in Mexico long before Spanish explorers arrived 500 years ago.

SOUTH AMERICA

DOMINICAN REPUBLIC

Many Dominicans have come to the U.S. to play baseball. One of them is home-run king Sammy Sosa!

SPAIN

Long ago, Spain was called Hispania, which means "land of rabbits." Ancient explorers gave it this name after finding a huge population of rabbits when they first visited the land.

ARGENTINA

ARGENTINA

Argentina was once the land of the dinosaur. The largest dinosaur ever discovered was found here. In 2001, a nest with thousands of dinosaur eggs was found. Move over, *Jurassic Park!*

PUERTO RICO

The island of Puerto Rico is a commonwealth of the U.S. That means that Puerto Ricans are U.S. citizens. Their president is the same as our current president. In Puerto Rico, people elect a governor, as in each state of the U.S.

Description

Reread "One Language, Many Nations." Fill in the graphic organizer with details about each kid.

We Are Latinos!

Kid's Name	Language Kid Speaks	Where Kid Is From	Interesting Fact About the Nation
Alina			
Thomas			
Robert			
Amanda			
Carlos			
Paula			

 Use the organizer above to retell "One Language, Many Nations" in your own words. Remember to include details about each kid and the place he or she is from.

Writing Frame

Use the information in your graphic organizer to fill in the writing frame. Write about Cuba, Mexico, Dominican Republic, and Puerto Rico.

Spanish is the common language of many places. This is because

_____

_____ .

In _____, Spanish is spoken. _____'s family came from

this nation. It _____ .

In _____, Spanish is spoken. _____'s family came from this

nation. It _____ .

In _____, Spanish is spoken. _____'s

family came from this nation. It _____

_____ .

In _____, Spanish is spoken. _____'s family came from

this nation. It_____ .

 Use the writing frame to tell about your classmates and their ancestors. Where necessary, change the word "Spanish" to the language spoken by the classmate's ancestors. Look in your social studies textbook if you need facts that will help you.

LET'S NAVIGATE

Follow the five easy steps when you read nonfiction text.

5 EASY STEPS

Step ① Preview
Read the title, introduction, and headings. Think about what they tell you.

Step ② Prepare
Say to yourself,
"This article is going to be about _____.
What do I already know?"

Step ③ Read
Carefully read the article.

Step ④ Use the Tools
Stop at special features, such as the special type and the graphics. Ask yourself,

- Why is this here?
- What does it tell me?
- How does it connect to the article?

Step ⑤ Retell/Connect
Retell what you learned. Think about how it connects to your life and the world.

①

THE AMAZING OCTOPUS

The octopus is an awesome ocean animal. It can be as HUGE as 30 feet or as tiny as 1 inch in length. What makes this creature so amazing?

Body Parts

③ An octopus has 8 arms that it uses to swim and to catch food. An octopus has suction cups on the back of its arms.

④ **Suction cups** help the octopus grab a meal, such as crabs, clams, and fish. If an octopus loses an arm, it can grow another one. This is called **regeneration** (ree-gen-uh-RAY-shun). A starfish can do the same thing.

An octopus has no bones, so its body is soft and squishy. This allows it to squeeze into small spaces. An octopus can squeeze into a seashell! This helps the octopus chase food even into little cracks.

Survival Skills

② Octopuses have many ways to avoid their enemies. An octopus can change colors as **camouflage** (KAM-uh-flahzh), a way to blend in with its surroundings. That way, its enemies can't see it. And, in the blink of an eye, it can make its skin bumpy. To an enemy, the octopus looks like just another rock!

An octopus can also squirt purple-black ink at its enemies. The enemy can't see the octopus through the ink, and the octopus can quickly swim away to safety.

⑤

SCHOLASTIC

TEXT STRUCTURES

Cause/ Effect

cause

effect

Problem/ Solution

problem

solution

Sequence

step 1 step 2 step 3 step 4

Description

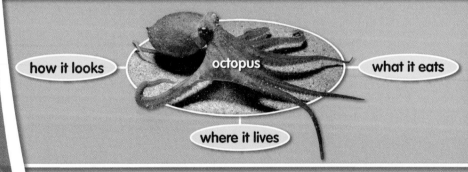
how it looks   octopus   what it eats

where it lives

Compare/ Contrast

land animals   both   water animals

Sequence

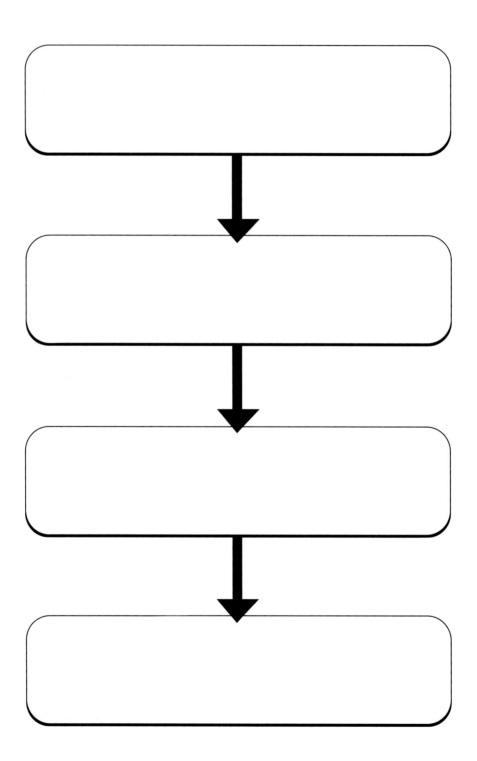

Compare/Contrast

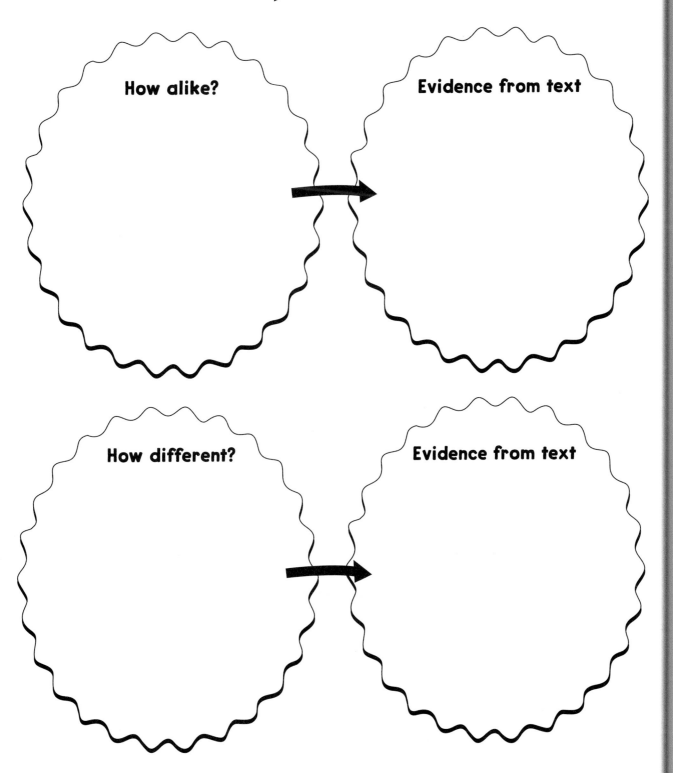

How alike?

Evidence from text

How different?

Evidence from text

Cause/Effect

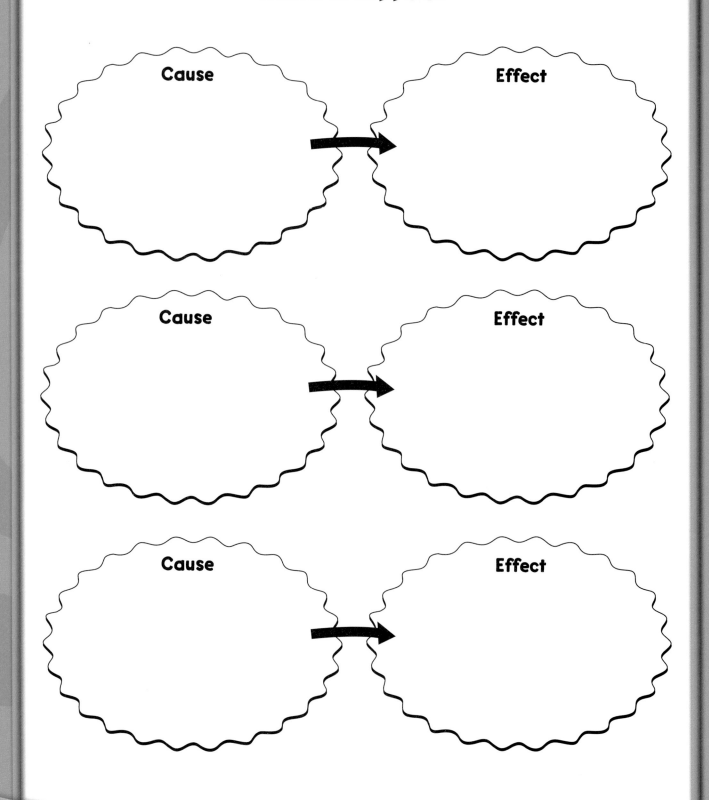

Cause → Effect

Cause → Effect

Cause → Effect

Problem/Solution

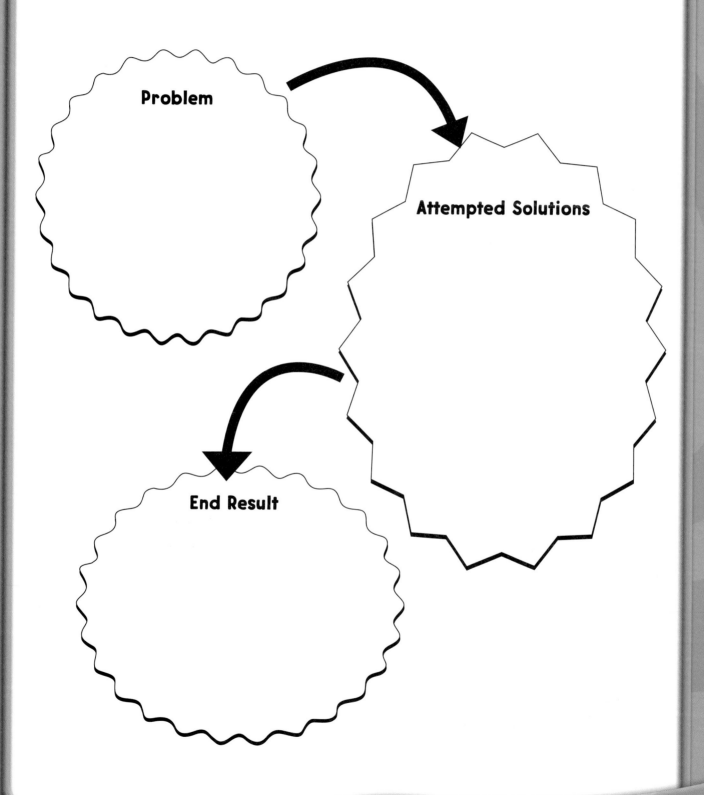

Problem

Attempted Solutions

End Result

Description

Main Idea _____

_____

Detail 1 _____

_____

Detail 2 _____

_____

Detail 3 _____

_____

Detail 4 _____

_____

Credits

Text: "Penguin Pullovers," "Marvelous Machines," "Robots Explore Extremes," "A New Museum," "Snow Dogs," "Kid Inventors," "Be Heart Smart!," "New Buzz on Bees," On Your Own article (page 16), "Mother Bear Man," On Your Own article (page 19), "Dino Time," "Life Underground," "Hot Spot," "Discover the Deep," "Problem Pets," "Animal Invaders," "Holiday Celebrations," "Thanksgiving: Myth and Fact," "It's Tornado Time," "New Animal Babies: New Hope for the Endangered," "Trunk Talk," "Sea Turtles on the Move," "Protect the Planet," "White House Firsts," "To Lead a New Nation," "A Son Remembers," "Native American State Names," "Chinese New Year," "Pluto Rocks!," "Helping Earth's Animals," "Powwow Now," "Hurricane Hunt," "One Language, Many Nations" are reprinted from SCHOLASTIC NEWS. Copyright © 1999, 2000, 2001, 2002, 2003, 2004 by Scholastic Inc. Reprinted by permission. "Blind Musher Takes on the Iditarod" is reprinted from SCHOLASTIC SCOPE. Copyright © 2005 by Scholastic Inc. Reprinted by permission. "Danger: High Speed!" is reprinted from SUPER SCIENCE. Copyright © 2001 by Scholastic Inc. Reprinted by permission. "Evergreen Cones Make Seeds" and "What Is a Food Chain?" are reprinted from CONTENT AREA READING: SCIENCE. Copyright © Scholastic. Reprinted by permission. "Why Do Communities Change?" and "The Mighty Mississippi River" are reprinted from CONTENT AREA READING: SOCIAL STUDIES. Copyright © Scholastic Inc. Reprinted by permission. "From Peanuts to Peanut Butter" is reprinted from MY FIRST BOOK OF HOW THINGS ARE MADE. Copyright © 1995 by Pond Press. Reprinted by permission. "Sports and Games" is adapted from AMERICAN HISTORY TIME LINES published by Scholastic Inc. Copyright © 1996 by Susan Washburn Buckley. Reprinted by permission.

Images: Cover: Bee © Michael Durham/Minden Pictures; White House © Craig Aurness/Corbis; Volcano © Jim Sugar/Corbis; Chinese Dragon © Dallas and John Heaton/Jupiter Images. Page 4: (clockwise from top) Mike Hutchings/Reuters; Kjell B. Sandved/Photo Researchers; Konrad Wothe/Minden. Page 5: (top) Gettyimages; (bottom) Shadow Robots Ltd. Page 7: (middle) Suzanne McCabe; (bottom) Smithsonian Institution/Museum of the American Indian. Page 8: (clockwise from top) Michael Crouser (2); Ken Graham/Ken Graham Agency; Kim Hecox/Ken Graham Agency. Page 9: AP. Page 10: Lisa Dunnack. Page 11: (top) Michael Marsal & Margret Winter; (bottom) Wild Planet Toys. Page 14: Teresa Southwell. Page 15: (clockwise from top left) AP; Dwight Kuhn; Robert & Linda Mitchell; Hans Pfletschinger/Peter Arnold. Page 17: (left) K.K. Amnann/Bruce Coleman; Mapman/Scholastic. Page 18: (left) Robert Caputo/Aurora Quanta; Mapman/Scholastic. Page 20: Valerie Jones/Discover Dinosaur Exhibition. Page 21: (photo) AP; (map & illustrations) Brian LaRossa. Page 24: Karen Beckhardt. Page 25: (clockwise from left): Mapman/Scholastic; Corbis; Ian Worpole. Page 26: OPS, LLC. Pages 27–28: Teresa Southwell. Page 29: Jason Robinson. Page 30: Bryon Thompson. Page 31: Nathan Hale. Page 35: (from top) David T. Roberts/Reuters; Jonathan Drake/Reuters; Scott Bauer/USDA; Brian LaRossa. Page 37: Robert Frerck/Odyssey Productions. Page 38: (from top) Ted Curtain/Plymouth Plantation (2); 2001 Russ Kendall FROM GIVING THANKS: The 1621 HARVEST FEAST, SCHOLASTIC PRESS. Page 40: AP. Page 41: (bottom) Mapman/Scholastic. Pages 44–45: David Coulson. Pages 47–48: Teresa Southwell. Page 49: Kelly Kennedy. Page 50: Peanut Association of America. Page 51: (top) David Coulson; (bottom) Brian LaRossa. Page 54: Natacha Pisarebko/AP; Mapman/Scholastic. Page 57: Gettyimages. Page 58: (clockwise from top) Brian LaRossa; Picture Quest; NASA. Page 59: (top) Brian LaRossa; (bottom) Lake County Museum/Corbis. Page 61: (clockwise from top left) Doug Perrine/Minden; Deroy/Minden; Alan Morgan/Peter Arnold; Ingrid Visser/Impact Visions; Mitsuaki/Minden; K. Atkinson/Animals Animals. Page 64: Brian LaRossa. Page 65: Corbis. Page 68: (top) Matthew Stockman/Gettyimages. Page 70: AP/Wide World Photos. Page 71: (left) Mapman/Scholastic; (right) Steve Allen/Picture Quest. Page 74: Copyright © 2007 Scholastic and its licensors. All rights reserved. Page 75: Granger. Page 77: David Coulson. Page 78: (top photo) Lillian Kohli; (bottom photo) Copyright © 2007 Scholastic and its licensors. All rights reserved; (illustrations) Teresa Southwell. Pages 80–81: Corbis. Page 85: (top) A. Ramey/PhotoEdit. Page 87: Digital Stock. Page 88: John R. Foster/Photo Researchers, Inc. Page 90: (from top) Garth Tilley/Gettyimages; Bob Daemmrich/The Imageworks; Young Wolf/PhotoEdit. Page 91: (from top) George Lepp/Gettyimages; Mary Clay/Gettyimages; Michael H. Francis. Page 94: Brian LaRossa. Page 95: (top) Kent Meireis/The Image Works; (bottom) Mapman/Scholastic. Page 96: Mapman/Scholastic. Page 97: Brian LaRossa. Page 98: Mapman/Scholastic. Pages 99–100: Brian LaRossa. Page 101: Mapman/Scholastic. Page 102: (from top) Jimmy Dorantes/Latin Focus.com; Lawrence Migdale; Jeff Greenberg/PhotoEdit; Laura Dwight/PhotoEdit; David Simeon/Stock Boston; Laura Dwight/PhotoEdit. Page 104: (from top) David Fleetham/Pacific Stock; © Mark Conlin/SeaPics.com; Eiichi Korasawa/Photo Researchers. Page 105: (from left to right) © Paul & Lindamarie Ambrose/Getty Images; © Albany Herald/Corbis Sygma; © Josef Beck/Getty Images; © Creatas/Jupiter Images; © Jim Zipp/Photo Researchers; © Jane Burton/Nature Picture Library; © Jef Meul/Foto Natura/Minden Pictures; © George McCarthy/Corbis; © Mark Conlin/SeaPics.com; © DLILLC/Corbis; © Brian Brown/Getty Images; © Tim McGuire/Corbis; © Royalty-Free/Corbis; © Martin Harvey/Corbis; © Gavriel Jecan/Corbis; © Denis Scott/Corbis; © Royalty-Free/Corbis; © Georgette Douwma/Gettyimages.

Editor: Mela Ottaiano
Cover Design: Jorge J. Namerow